THE MONK WHO LIVED AGAIN

Fray Luis at last a full-fledged Dominican Friar

THE MONK WHO
LIVED AGAIN

by

B. H. PEARSON

Published in the United States of America by
COWMAN PUBLICATIONS, INC.

Published in Great Britain by
CHRISTIAN LITERATURE CRUSADE,
LONDON

CHRISTIAN LITERATURE CRUSADE
106A Church Road, London, S.E.19

U.S.A.

Fort Washington, Pa.

Australia

243 Pitt Street, Sydney N.S.W.

New Zealand

174 Arthur Street, Onehunga, Auckland

also in

Europe, Australia, North America,
Central America, South America,
West Indies, Africa, India,
Indonesia, Far East

New Edition 1958
Reprinted 1962
Reprinted 1965

Printed in Great Britain by
Fletcher & Son Ltd, Norwich

DEDICATED

to

DR. WALTER MANUEL MONTANO

a "Saint Paul" of Latin America, and Esther Piper Montano, his wife, who has laboured so faithfully at his side; and their beautiful children, Betty, "Junior", and Edmund.

CONTENTS

FOREWORD

By the Rev. A. Stuart McNairn of the E.U.S.A.

IN the year 1898 there went from the town of Reading, England, to Peru a young missionary couple to work in the ancient City of the Sun, Cuzco, the capital of the one-time Inca Empire. A saintly mother, as she said goodbye to her boy, pledged herself to work with him by prayer, and her prayers were guided by the vivid letters telling of conditions, difficulties, and triumphs in that land. Ere long the mother was saddened but deeply moved by the descriptions of the power of the priests and their bitter opposition to the gospel, and she set herself to pray for the conversion of one of these priests, realizing what a power such a man might wield for God if brought into the Light.

One sad day brought the news that her boy had been called to higher service, and that the widow and her two little children were on their way back to the homeland. But this staggering blow did not turn her from her part in the work he had begun, and she continued to pray that God would give her a priest for that land.

The years passed, and another young couple was sent out to carry on the work so ably begun by her own children, and her great mother-heart adopted these two as her children in the work of the gospel. But still she prayed for a priest.

There came a day after many years of prayer when her adopted son wrote with joy that her prayers had been answered and they had now in their ranks a converted priest, a Spanish priest, a cultured man, an ex-professor of the University of Santander in Spain, and now mighty in the gospel. But the old Reading mother wrote back to say that although she thanked God, this was not her priest; he was not of the land. And she continued to pray.

Then one day she received a letter telling of the conversion of a young Franciscan monk from one of the monasteries who had given himself to God and was doing wonderful itinerant

Bible-selling and preaching in and around Cuzco. True, he was of Austrian birth, but he had been converted in Cuzco; was this her answer? No, she said; that was not her priest. And she continued steadfast in prayer.

At last there came a notable night in the city of Cuzco when, in the dark hour that precedes the dawn, a figure in the gloomy robes of a Dominican monk stole out of the ancient monastery that stands where once stood the Golden Temple of the Sun and made his way through the silent streets to the mission house where prayer was wont to be made, and the gospel preached; and the missionary, called from his bed to admit the sinister figure, found a despairing soul seeking God and the peace of God if haply they might be found. After five hours' talk and prayer he had the joy of seeing a priest of the land yield his heart to Christ and take what proved to be a hard and bitter cross to follow Him.

This book, *The Monk Who Lived Again*, tells how one New Year's morning a babe was born in a cultured and deeply religious home in the far Andes, how the babe grew to boyhood and manhood, was educated for the priesthood, looked to find God in the shelter of the Church, and found only evil and hypocrisy; how his hunger for God and for peace haunted and hounded him, and how at last he found both in Christ his Saviour.

The point of this brief foreword to a remarkable book is that, though impossible to fix dates to a matter of days, that New Year's morning when the little babe, destined to become a priest, was born in the far land of the Incas, was as nearly as can be traced the very time that the old Reading mother began to lay hold upon God for a priest from among the people to whom her boy had given his life. And, though in ways neither she nor anyone else would have dreamed, God began to answer her prayer, and unto us a child was born; and to-day, though his prayer-mother has gone to her rest, he is serving as she hoped he would, a mighty power for God, and reaching, both by voice and pen, multitudes who would never hear the gospel through the ordinary missionary channels.

PRELUDE

THIS our story, let it here be said, does not refer directly or indirectly to the Roman Catholic religion except as it exists in Latin America. It is only fair to that faith to say that there are millions within that Church in those southern lands, as elsewhere, who lament the almost unbelievable medievalism which forms the background of this true tale of South America and who would welcome a reformation from within the Roman Church; but the small minority who are in control have thus far refused any modifications except when compelled by civil law to do so, as in the case of the abolition of the Inquisition. Many millions in these lands, rebelling against church conditions, have become atheists.

This story of "Fray Luis", as Dr. Walter Manuel Montano* was known for seven years, can be thoroughly documented, and while not written as history, is true to facts. While no one would claim exactness in recalling dialogue of years past and childhood scenes, yet as carefully as possible the reader is assisted in living this eventful life. Lying back of this simple tale are such an abundance of letters, official documents and press dispatches that here even reference to them cannot be made. Many personal names, titles, even localities which would lend colour and depth to the story have been eliminated to make easier reading for those understanding only English.

If hearts are encouraged to see that the blood and treasure spent in sending the gospel to South America during years past have not been in vain; if young men and young women today can be challenged to give their best for the redemption of this great world of Latin America; if volunteers for service in this "Other America" will but offer themselves for this "last frontier"—then shall the purposes of this story have been fulfilled.

B. H. P.

LOS ANGELES, CALIFORNIA, JULY 1940.

* Pronounced MON-TAN-YO.

CHAPTER ONE

BEHIND CLOSED DOORS

THE monastery of Santo Domingo was wrapped in the intense cold of early morning. Utter silence reigned within its black-grey walls which loomed ponderously above the city of Cuzco, Peru, and which, outlined by the stars, seemed as eternal as the near-by Andes.

Within the darkness of his unlighted cell Fray Luis was standing motionless behind the door which opened out on to the large inner *patio*. For him this night had been an unending agony. It was not alone the danger, the physical strain; but a spiritual battle, still unwon, raged in his soul.

At times through the night there had come to him in startling vividness a vision of the time when he had consecrated himself upon the altars of the church—the swelling music of the organ, the voices of the massed choir of monks, the clouds of incense, the reverence of the throngs which crowded the chapel. But now, what lay ahead of him? Ignominy? Hatred of family and friends? Persecution? Death? Perhaps he was jumping headlong from one hell into a deeper one, just as the lost souls of Dante's *Inferno* wandered from one torment to another.

He suddenly remembered his father, patrician of ancient lineage, scholar and gentleman-born, Regent of the University of Cochabamba—the students called him "Kaiser". Yes, what would he say and do? What of his uncle, Eliodoro Villazon, venerable head of the renowned family clan, former President of Bolivia? What shame, perhaps, he was now bringing upon a name which for a hundred years and more had stood for all that was best in the life of the nation, and even now was a magic wand to open all doors. Yes, all doors except those of this monastery! Would they despise him, hate him? Well, it made no difference now. It was too late to think of that. Nothing could be worse than what had been. He had nothing to lose but his life. All else was already lost.

Fray Luis looked instinctively towards the wall where he knew Holy Mary, the Virgin of the Rosary, was hanging. In the semi-darkness of his room he could still picture to himself the fresh, rosy cheeks of her who, aside from Saint Domingo, had been his only companion for the seven years past. How often he had felt her smile upon him, sensed her spirit speaking to his, thrilled to her presence in the long hours of his loneliness. And yet she, too, had failed him, mocked him, deceived him. A bitter smile crept over his face.

The young man strained forward in the darkness, listening intently. As he shifted his weight from one foot to another a board creaked beneath him. The sound was, of course, communicated to the priests' cells which extended east and west from his room along the north side of the building. The prior himself must certainly have heard. The thought of the prior drove all other fears from his mind. This man was no metaphysical concept like the devil, hell, or demons—he was a very real man of energy who left to no blind providence the meting out of punishments and rewards. For the spiritual head of a Christian order, what a perverse genius he was. Able to jest and drink with the drunken, to reason with the learned, to discipline his monks with an iron hand—a model ecclesiastic, Fray Luis thought wryly.

Silence pervaded the building save for a morning breeze, born on the condor-inhabited heights of the Andes, which sighed softly about the eaves and swept a rustling murmur from the palms in the *patio*. For a moment it flashed through his mind that the grey, grim monastery, as well as the towering, inaccessible Andes which rose sheer above the city, formed parts of one great eternity, and here through this eternity he, his friends, his family, all of South America, stood in the darkness before a closed door that should never open. Yes, he had been standing for an eternity behind those doors which never opened. The doors of social caste and obligation had bound him as a lad. The doors of religious pride and devotion had locked him away from youth's usual pursuits. The doors of this monastery had closed behind him, shutting out the daylight of normal life, leaving him in the region of the living dead. Doors, locked doors, doors in his own mind, doors in his heart, doors he had been unable to open, for which he could find no key, had always held him prisoner. And always just outside those closed doors was the fear of social ostracism, of ecclesiastical excommunication, of the devil or the prior, or hell. But those doors were all being pushed open at once now.

Dawn was coming up over the Andes; the light was glowing brighter each moment. He felt the sun-rise in his own soul. He would be master of his own destiny. He was bursting open the door of the monastery—defying priest, acolyte, cardinal, and pope. For good or ill another destiny awaited him beyond that door.

But what, after all, if that door before him should silently open and the prior step in, flash on the lights, discover his preparations for flight, break forth in a flood of Spanish invective, order him to a prison cell? There, was another friar who had tried escape. He was sent to France. Yes, France had a most effective way of dealing with ecclesiastical criminals. They never escaped; they never talked; they never wrote. They disappeared as quietly as a white cloud on a summer morning in a torrid desert—for the glory of the Church. France or Rome, either would be terrible enough! Rome, after all, was perhaps most to be dreaded, though he knew less about what happened to one there. As for that matter, in their own Dominican jail, hidden away in the underground recesses of this very monastery, one could spend a lifetime and be lost for ever to friends and family. Fear, as some impalpable wind off fields of snow, chilled him into a slight shiver. He felt his heart pause for a second with new dread which sent weakness pulsating through his body.

In the first grey light of early dawn he could make out the Virgin's image faintly. Instinctively he crossed himself. Now, if ever, was her time to act. Why did she not come down from the wall, if she could—speak to him, save him? She did not move, and yet in the soft, strange light of dawn he felt uncannily that someone was in the room with him. Restlessly his eyes searched out the deeper shadows.

How many times when he had longed for another hour to sleep the young man whose task it was each morning to awaken the monks had come too soon. Now he waited impatiently. When he came action would take the place of this horrible suspense. He had done penance kneeling on peach pips until prayer had become an agony—but what was that compared with a night like this? He might have gone to bed, but that would have meant movement, and movement meant noise. No, better to stand there by the closed door, ready, waiting, rather than risk failure.

At last he heard the rattle of keys in a distant lock. A moment later bells in the town were ringing out the call to morning worship. Footsteps were sounding down the corridor outside the row of cells. "Let us bless the Lord" (*Benedicamus Domino*), boomed the voice of the awakener, as he pounded upon the monks' doors. Fray Luis wondered if, when he replied, his voice would betray his intense excitement. But the man stood just outside his door now, thumping upon it heartily. In as sleepy tones as possible he responded from within, "Thanks be to God!" (*Deo Gratias*). The man passed on down the gallery and turned on the far side of the building, his voice becoming fainter in the distance, leaving behind him only the soft ripple of the monks dressing.

As Fray Luis knew, the awakener came at half past four. At five o'clock the monks at a signal bell would step out into the gallery and start marching to the loft facing the great altar, where an hour and a half would be spent at morning prayers. Less than thirty minutes were his for carrying out his plan of action. If he failed—but he must not fail.

Swiftly he opened the door. He reached down and picked up his two leather cases, carefully packed with needed clothing, and above all else the precious manuscripts which were the fruit of these buried years within monastery walls.

With his shoes tucked under his arm he followed as noiselessly as possible the gallery which ran in front of the monks' cells. He must pass the room of the choirmaster (*Maestro de Coristas*). Perhaps it was nervousness, or it may have been that after the first few steps he grew careless, for as he passed the doorway of this august representative of a tyrannous God, one of his shoes slid from beneath his arm and clattered down upon the flagstones with a noise that, to his ears, boomed guiltily throughout the great edifice.

He stood frozen in his tracks. Should he fly swiftly to the retreat of his cell, leaving the tell-tale shoes behind him? If the master's door opened suddenly, as it seemed it certainly must, what story could he tell to cover his crime? For a moment he waited noiselessly, then stooped, picked up the offending shoe, and hurried on through the richly carved door of the Chapel of the Virgin of the Rosary, crossed its sacred floor, scarce daring to raise his eyes to the saints looking on in horrified silence, then out into the larger *patio* where the fruit trees grew.

Silently he made his way down the flagstones of the inner porch or gallery, around the ghostly shapes of the trees and shrubs, grey-green in the dim light of the morning. Quickly he went through the doorway out into the church grounds, down past the great hewn rocks which once were the foundations of the Temple of the Sun in Inca days, to where the boy with the keys for the outer doors was sleeping. There were still more doors that he must open. The thirty minutes were already well-spent, and this meant life or death for him.

Breathing heavily, Fray Luis stopped before a stone stairway leading up a few feet to a modern door which had been placed over an ancient opening in the stone wall, and set down his leather bags. Softly he called, "Heh, Pedro! Heh, Pedro! Wake up! Come; it is time to open the doors!"

There was no answer. He picked up a few pebbles from beside the path and tossed them against the door. Always doors and more doors to be opened! "Pedro, open!" he commanded.

"Yes, Father, I am coming!" replied a voice from within.

"But what is the hurry, Father?" asked the lad as he opened the door and sleepily started down towards the waiting monk. All at once he caught sight of the large suitcases at the friar's side and his doctor's cap upon his head. "Why, Fray Luis, what does this mean?" he asked in startled wonderment. Then as the full realization of what was happening came over him he dropped to his knees, took the monk's hand and, kissing it, pleaded, "Oh, Father you cannot, you must not do this! Why Father, you, the most beloved of all our chapter! How can you do this? Go back, please go back! I will help you! Quick, you must do it!"

"Get up! Get up at once, Pedro! There is no time to lose. You must obey me at once. You do not understand. I am obeying a higher law. Take these bags and carry them for me. You shall be rewarded for this. This is God's will."

Mechanically the boy, as always, obeyed a friar's command. Lifting the heavily-laden suitcases the lad started down the walk past the ancient remains of the Temple of the Sun. In a few minutes the monks would be assembling in the choir at the far end of the chapel. Fray Luis and Pedro must make their way directly through the entire length of this building before the priests' devotions began.

B

In a moment the boy in front of him opened the door into the church and stood back for him to pass. As Fray Luis stepped within, his heart almost failed him. The white-robed members of the Dominican Order were filing into the loft. Despite the dimness of the morning light which filtered through the stained-glass windows, he felt that they could not fail to see him. But his only safety now lay in going forward. Dragging the boy after him, he stepped into a near-by confessional box and waited, trembling with excitement. He had to think a way out of this. He could not go back. And yet, as he must walk the entire length of the building under the gaze of the monks, if he went forward how avoid discovery?

"Father——" began the boy.

"Keep quiet, Pedro," Fray Luis replied impatiently. "You know nothing about this."

Suddenly he grabbed Pedro's arm. "Come at once!" he ordered. "And silently!"

He darted out of the confessional box, pushing the lad before him. He had seen the priests lay their heads upon their folded arms. He knew the length of that prayer. It would carry them safely under the shadow of the choir loft which held the praying friars. They had reached the exit as the monotonous level tones of the prayer continued.

Once more Pedro dropped to his knees, "Father, you must not——" he began.

"Get up, Pedro! I love you, lad, and you have been good to me. See, I trust you. Fray Luis puts all confidence in you. I know that you love me, son of my soul, and that is why I trust you. Open the door, Pedrito!"

Fray Luis had quickly pulled on his shoes. He stooped to pick up his cases. Something had happened. Either they were much heavier than when he had started that morning, or else —yes, no doubt that was it—the strain of the night was telling on him. The nervous shocks of the last thirty minutes as he trembled between a living death in a Dominican cell, and free-dom, had robbed him of his strength. He staggered as he tried to lift them. He could not carry both. He would take the one with his personal effects and his beloved manuscripts—to lose them would be like losing his life. For the other things he could come later.

"Take this; keep it, Pedro! It is mine. No one shall see

it, touch it, until I return. They will punish you if you show it to them. I will return later for it. You understand? Keep it as a mark of your love for me and of Fray Luis' confidence in Pedro. You will be faithful, I know."

Tears were streaming down the boy's face. He picked up the hand which set down the heavy suitcase and kissed it affectionately and as a sign of fealty, then turned and opened the doors with the heavy, ornate key which hung at his side.

Fray Luis made the sign of the cross in blessing, and stepped out through the doorway into the chill air of an early dawn in Cuzco. The cool wind from off the towering Andes seemed to give him strength.

The priests in the choir overhead were chanting "My God! My God! Why hast Thou forsaken me? Why art Thou so far from helping me, and from the words of my roaring?"

Though he did not know it then, Fray Luis was hurrying down Santo Domingo Street towards the great adventure of his life.

CHAPTER TWO

THE MAKING OF A MONK

THE aristocratic suburb where the home of Dr. German
Guillen Montano was located is a place of almost continuous springtime. It is surrounded by wooded hills which
lead to the blue-brown heights of the Andes, seeming always
so near as quite to environ those who live there, and yet so
remotely aloof in their majestic strength as to remain always
the mysterious domain of the Indian who broods upon the
glories of the past. From this district one may look down upon
the red-tiled roofs of scattered dwellings which lie in the
purple distance of the valley and, to the south, the shining
white walls of the buildings of beautiful, dreamy Cochabamba, the jewel city of Bolivia.

On a certain spring afternoon in the early part of this
twentieth century Master Walter Manuel Montano, youngest
son of Dr. German Guillen Montano, sat with all the seriousness becoming a future friar upon the knees of an Indian
servant girl. She was dressed in the multi-coloured native dress
of five or six skirts, each a different, rich, primitive hue which
only peoples of great natural dignity and charm can wear.
The boy placed his chubby hands upon her high cheekbones
and commanded autocratically, with the calm assurance of a
four-year-old who knows that he will be obeyed, "Again!
again! Tell me *the* story!"

The use of the Indian language had been forbidden within
the home lest the boy should fail to appreciate the beautiful
cadences of the Spanish; but, as for him, he had already determined to spurn the official tongue of his parents in favour of
an idiom which brought to him so many delightful tales of
long-ago times, and in this he was aided and abetted by his
brown-eyed nurse. *The* story could be no other, and slowly,
in tones which carried conviction, the Indian girl began, in
the dialect of her own mountain highlands, the tale her young
charge had ordered:

"When Manco Capac and Mama Ocllo first came to Peru,
these fathers of the Incas brought with them a wedge of purest

20

gold. They were seeking a place to build their royal city, a city where they should have their throne, for the sun-god had told them that they must travel on and on, ever southward, until the magic, gold wedge should fly from their hands and bury itself in the earth—there they should build the palace of our great Indian empire.

"So on and on they went, carrying the magic, golden wedge in their hands. But never did it move. They could not find the place for their royal city. They came down the shore-line of Peru where the mighty ocean is, but the magic, golden wedge did not move. They crossed over the fertile plains which carry one to the mountains, and the golden, magic wedge lay still in their hands. They started up the great Andean Mountains, on whose peaks the snow rests and at whose feet the fountains and rivers spring forth, but nothing happened.

"At times they were discouraged and wondered if the prophecy were true that their wise men had told them of the magic of the golden wedge, when one day they came to what we now call Cuzco. Suddenly they felt the magic, golden wedge stir in their hands. They tried to hold it, but they could not. It flew away and hovered for a moment in the air like a golden bird, and then they saw it plunge down into the ground and disappear.

"Falling upon their knees they gave thanks to the great sun-god, and there it was they placed the temple of their father, the sun. They built it out of the golden tears of the sun which he had shed for the sufferings they endured. It was a temple of purest gold—Coricancha, the glory of the Indians—their throne was gold, their palace of gold; for there it was the golden wedge revealed its magic."

The lad settled down into the folds of his Indian nurse's purple dress and leaned confidingly back against her breast, which was covered with a red-and-white jacket buttoned about her. Over either shoulder a heavy braid of black hair, thrown forward, formed a frame for the quiet, serious boy.

"When I grow up," said the little master of the home in perfect Indian dialect, sighing delightedly, "I will find a magic, golden wedge, and it will guide me, too, and I will build a royal city." He gazed out with the fixed eyes of dreaming childhood when the visions of future glory first come, and the Indian girl bent forward to kiss his tumbled tresses.

Both nurse and child had been oblivious of the approach
of a well-dressed lady of rather haughty bearing. Her skilfully
arranged coiffure of dark brown hair was drawn back from
her high but narrow forehead, and her dark eyes flashed with
indignation as she overheard the lad's remark.

"What is this, Maria?" she cried angrily in Spanish. "Talking once more that filthy language of the mountains. Have
I not told you that it is forbidden in my home? Use Spanish
or do not speak at all!"

"Don't say that, my stepmother!" cried the boy imperi-
ously, sliding down off the Indian woman's knees and facing
the newcomer. "This is an *Indian* story!"—as though that
should explain the matter.

The Spanish woman, with a contemptuous toss of her head,
reached down and took the boy by the hand, jerking him towards the other end of the corridor. "You come with me," she
said with a note of finality. "As for you, Maria, get on with
your work, and don't let me hear you talking that vulgar
language of the mountains any more."

Dragging young Walter Manuel after her, she opened a
door out on to a low terrace overlooking a large yard filled
with tropical fruit trees and bright-coloured flowering shrubs.
"You stay out there and play," the woman ordered severely.
"I do not want my house littered up with your things and the
furniture all disarranged." The door was slammed behind
him decisively. Walter Manuel stood looking back at the closed
door ruefully. Why were there so many doors in the world? he
wondered. Some day he himself would open and shut doors.
That would be much better. Until then he must wait and,
whatever he thought, do as others expected. The limits of the
garden *patio* in which he had been placed were definitely
marked by a high wall, above which he could see a cascade
of water pouring down the near-by mountainside.

In the shade of a large Cherimoya tree sat a distinguished-
looking gentleman at a table, reading with deep absorption.
His broad forehead betokened a mind disposed to philosophy;
the serious cast of his face indicated the scholar; the sharply
disciplined moustachios helped to account perhaps for the
nickname which the boys at the Cochabamba University had
given him—"Kaiser". Young Walter Manuel walked towards
the man, who remained unconscious of his presence.

"Hello, Daddy!" said the little fellow, laying a hand expectantly upon the man's knee.

The father did not lift his eyes from the pages of the book before him. "Yes, yes, my son. How are you?" he said, mechanically, in acknowledgement of the greeting, continuing his reading.

"Daddy, I want to play," the lad urged. "Won't you play with me?"

"Yes, yes, my son," the man answered, turning a page of his book. "Yes, surely, you must play. How are you, my son?"

"Daddy, tell me, is Mama still asleep?" asked the wee bit of humanity.

Something seemed to have disturbed the composure of the man; his attention loosened from the pages before him like ice from a pavement when the spring sun strikes it. He laid the volume down and turned to the lad, taking his two small hands in his own. The boy bowed his head as a matter of course and kissed his father's hands. "What was that you asked?" inquired the man in the clear, sonorous Castillian of the patrician bred and born.

"Is Mama still asleep?" inquired the boy again.

"Yes, yes. She is still asleep. It is too late now; she will never awaken. She was most beautiful, young and beautiful, though the mother of my five children. She was warm and tender and smiling, filled with love for everyone. I needed her, son, and most of all you needed her, too. I do not know why she was taken. But the priest tells us we must not question the doings of divine providence." He crossed himself instinctively.

"I have many duties, my son, as Regent of the University. There are many books to read and many papers to write. Some day you will understand." He dropped the lad's hands and turned back to the volume which he had laid face down upon the table, and once more quickly entered the realm of thought in which he lived.

"I want to play," demanded the little fellow wistfully; "I want somebody to play with me."

The father raised his eyes from his book and glanced swiftly at the titles of the volumes before him. Selecting one, he handed it to his son. "Take that," he directed. "This will be your play. Read that. You must read. You must study. You must be a learned man and a gentleman." With this the man turned back to his book once more, receding again from the world of reality.

As the lad started off carrying the heavy tome he announced gravely, "I wish I were an Indian!"

Gradually the tension in the home increased. The step-mother, never having had any children of her own, knew exactly what children should be. Walter Manuel, she found, failed at many points. He sometimes tramped dirt into the house. Sometimes he ruffled the rich, beautiful rugs which lay in exact pattern across the polished, hardwood floors. Once he opened the cage where the songbirds were, permitting them to escape. This first attempt at opening doors was far from what he thought success should be. He had even threatened the safety of the goldfish in their large glass bowl, and alto-gether he was a most insanitary, unnecessary interruption in the rhythm of a well-ordered home. So it was that a change in residence was determined for the lad. Not long afterwards his father took him to the home of Father Ledezma, the lead-ing Catholic authority of the district, a learned man and a professor in the seminary (*Seminario Conciliar*) and, what is more to the point, Walter Manuel's uncle.

"But you must stay here, son," said the father in answer to his son's insistent questions. They turned into the walk of one of the most imposing homes in Cochabamba. "You will be happier here, and I will come often to see you. Father Ledezma is a man of learning. Your mother would wish it so if she could speak to us."

The word "mother" opened a flood of memories to Walter Manuel. He could still recall the tenderness of her love; those arms open to receive him; the warm breasts against which he nestled, secure from all misfortune; the sweet, unmeaning words so full of meaning; of the lullaby songs with which she quieted his childish fears and led him into drowsy land. But she was asleep and would never awaken. One must make the best of life as one found it. Still, home is home, and one's father is one's father, for all he is Regent and State Secretary of Education.

Father Ledezma was indeed a most excellent man. Walter Manuel was most cordially received by the stout, big-faced priest. Every attention was showered upon him, and he was made to feel that he was most welcome in the two-storied colonial mansion. As his father waved him goodbye he felt doubtless much as little Samuel did when Hannah left him in Eli's care.

Walter Manuel Montano's first duties in the priesthood were assigned him by Father Ledezma. Each afternoon the poor came to the home of the priest to beg. The boy was plentifully supplied with ten-cent pieces and given the duty of tossing one from the second-storey balcony to all who might request aid. It was thrilling business for the lad.

But not having yet become versed in the sacrosanct character of the social caste to which he belonged and which enforced its obligations upon its own members with unyielding rigour, he one day decided that he would hand the money to the needy rather than toss it through the air at them.

Without consulting anyone Walter Manuel came down from the balcony and stood on the steps of the house where the people gathered around him admiring his clothing, patting his head, and talking interminably of how wise he was, how "pretty" he was, of how great a man he would be, and of their great love for him. He was too young to know that the mere change in level from which largesse is administered is sufficient to stay the tides of revolution or precipitate a reign of terror. He only knew that it pleased him to have them crowd around him and shower pretty names and titles upon him, and place in their hands the coin which should bring some relief to their dull, hard life. It was not long until they were bringing rude, home-made toys to him, which he received with befitting dignity. Without understanding it in the least, he was on the way to becoming a political, or was it religious, boss in his own right. But he was breaking the "code", though he knew it not.

One day his uncle, priest of Cochabamba as well as Cathedral Professor (*Canonigo Catedralico*), discovered the boy surrounded by his beggar friends. "Come here," he ordered the boy in tones which scattered the admiring group; and grasping him by the arm, he led him through the door which closed behind them, shutting out the "rabble". When they were alone he taught the boy, "Gentlemen must not contaminate themselves by contact with low people like this. They are but

swine and beggars and can never be anything else. You are a
gentleman and you must behave like one. No more of such
actions as these. *Dios mio*, son! You were letting them touch
you, and some of those dirty women were hugging you. Phih!
You should have known better!''

After this first lesson in priestly aloofness the money was
tossed from the balcony once more.

Occasionally the motonony of the days would be broken by
a visit to the home of Uncle Eliodoro Villazon, former President of Bolivia. With grey moustache and neatly-trimmed
beard, eyes still bright, deep set in a sea of wrinkles as though
in dropping into place they had rippled the calm surface of
his face into smiles, he seemed like a bit of living history, so
long ago was it that he had wisely and ably guided the destinies of the nation.

One day as the old gentleman balanced his nephew, Walter
Manuel, upon his knee he unfolded to him the story of his
family history. ''More than one hundred and fifty years ago,''
began Eliodoro Villazon, with the slow, careful emphasis of a
man who is accustomed to weighing his words in public, ''the
founder of our family was privileged to risk his life for the
King of Spain. Because of the victory which he won that day
the king gave to him the wonderful Castle Guillen and ordered
a special shield to be made for him, and a coat-of-arms which
no one else might use, and the Guillen Castle became known
everywhere as our family home.

''As the sons grew to manhood and had families of their
own, they and all their children were permitted to add 'del
Castillo Guillen' to their name, so that all might know they
were honoured by the king. And you, my son, are one of these,
which is for you both an honour and a responsibility, for
all your forebears have been brave men and patriots, and many
of them have died in defence of the truth.''

''But we do not serve the King of Spain today,'' the boy
objected. ''How then can we use a name which the King of
Spain gave to us?''

''Well,'' answered the old patriarch, shifting the lad to the
other knee, ''I will tell you again how this came to be. After
the Spanish conquerors, Pizarro and Valverde, had over-
thrown the Empire of the Incas and had taken Upper Peru,
which today we know as our own beloved Bolivia, one of our

family was sent to what is now our own beautiful city of Cochabamba on a special commission from the Spanish Crown.

"So enchanted was he with the beauties of nature and the geniality of the people that he asked permission to settle here. Land was given to him by the Crown, special privileges were conferred upon him, and he was the first of our family in New Spain. His children married among the finest families, and here, too, the name 'Guillen' became a power.

"But there was also much evil in this New Spain. The great republic of the United States had just been formed in the north. The spirit of democracy and liberty had arisen, with its cry of liberty, equality, and fraternity. The conscience of the world was stirred. Mexico was in the throes of her revolution. Soldiers were marching in our land. Bolivar and San Martin, the great heroes of our history, were rousing the whole continent to fight for our liberties. Our family must choose. There was no middle ground. While we were tied by wealth, tradition, culture, and favours to the Crown of Spain, still stronger was our love of liberty and our interest in the masses. So it is that when you read the history of the independence of Bolivia you will find among her heroes many of your great-great-great-grandparents and their children."

"Yes, yes!" shouted the little fellow excitedly, his eyes shining, "I know them all. I have seen them many times, there in the Museum of Cochabamba, with their bright, beautiful uniforms, their jewels and swords, their medals and ribbons—what wonderful men they are! Some day I, too, will be a soldier."

The grand old gentleman of Bolivia, Dr. Eliodoro Villazon, laughed so uproariously at the enthusiasm of his little friend that tears rolled down his cheeks. "Certainly! Of course you will! Rascal that you are! But, after all, whom will you fight?"

The boy slid down off his uncle's knee and faced him with blazing eyes. His arms swung with the natural rhythm of the born orator. "Whom will I fight? Why should not our blood flow again? Can we ever forget the vile war of 1879 when cowardly Chile, robber that she is, took our great saltpetre beds?* Bah! I hate them! I could fight them today! Some

* In Antofagasta and Mejillones.

day I shall fight. Gladly shall our land have my life. Down with Chile!" He stamped his foot in most approved fashion just as he had seen the orators in the parks do on patriotic days. So many times had he heard the denunciation of their sister republic, Chile, in the family circle or in the classes at school that like all true Bolivians, young and old, he could deliver an oration of war and hate against their ancient enemy at a moment's notice.

"Come, now," said Señor Villazon, smiling in a spirit of *camaraderie* as he laid his hand upon the boy's shoulder, "of a truth I fear that you will be going to war. But still there are many opportunities open to you, little one. I am counting on you to carry on the traditions of our family. Remember that today among your relatives are governors, judges, mayors, teachers, ecclesiastics, congressmen, physicians, lawyers, honourable men all. In your veins there flows the blood of Mariano Baptista, the famed golden-tongued orator-statesman who served as president of Bolivia before my day. You must be worthy of these!"

The lad saluted gravely as he said, "At your orders, my uncle!"

But one day when Dr. German Guillen Montano came to see his son, love of home was too strong for Walter Manuel. He threw his arms around his father's neck and refused to be separated from him.

"You will not be happy at home, my son," said the distraught man. "What will you do with the stepmother? She is a good woman, but she does not know children, poor thing! And you, how can you understand? For you are so young."

But the lad clung desperately to him. He took the boy with him because he must, but to neither a home nor a mother. That is perhaps the reason for the choices which later shaped his strange destiny.

CHAPTER THREE

THE WAY OF CAIN

As the years slipped by, Walter Manuel ceased to be a child and became a youth. Of one thing there could be no doubt—he was religious. Baptized at birth by the bishop, regular attendant at Confession and Mass, of which he partook with the greatest fear and the most religious fervour, as one who knew the wafer host to be the very body, soul, and Passion of Christ—deity itself, in fact—in him the Roman Catholic Church could be assured of a devotee whose loyalty might not be questioned.

If the full truth were spoken, he might have been said to be unusually religious, and this, as many a doubter has sagely observed, is or may be a most serious thing in one's life. In the first place, he had no playtime, as most youngsters have, and, shut up within the great *patio* or the spacious house not meant for youth to live in, but whose every room reminded one of art, learning, or the classic wisdom of the past; with the example of his father, whom he never saw except when engrossed in some heavy tome of learning, or writing with the furious industry of a philosopher who knows that his time on earth is limited—what more natural than that he, too, should tend to the search for truth? And that, after all, is religion, as the prophets of all ages have told us.

But more than this, more even than the daily tolling of the cathedral bells, the solemnity of the Confessional, the sacred fear of the Mass, the inspired music which reminded one of eternity, the stained-glass windows which infused one's very soul with light, the saints who surrounded one with their hallowed influence, there was something still deeper, more elemental, which drove him into the life of the Church. He had been denied something. He had never known a mother's love, a mother's tenderness, except in that vague period of infancy, with its fading memory of one, the only one, who ever really seemed to care. A father, some fathers, might have supplied this loss. But not Dr. German Guillen Montano. It would have

made one smile just a bit to think of "The Kaiser" attempting
to take a mother's place.

And so it was that as a child Walter Manuel, who had not
known a mother's arms, turned instinctively to God. God
cared for one. God had arms—Christ had, at least—how
tenderly He had lifted the children and blessed them as He
held them against His breast. He was dead, of course. But God
had a Mother, Mary, the Mother of God—she was alive, she
was our intercessor, our mediator, our refuge, our succour;
she was our very "present help in time of trouble", the
"Queen of Heaven", our Mother, our holy Mother. She would
hear his prayers; she actually smiled down at him from where
her softly-lighted image was placed above the altar in the
church. She had done wonderful miracles—for others, in distant places. He, too, would find refuge within those cosmic
arms of the "Queen of Heaven", and pillow his head on the
breast where the little Child Jesus had lain in innocent sleep.

As he grew older he determined that, as in all things else,
so in religion he would be positive. If religion were what it
claimed to be, then it mattered more than all beside. He knew
this must be so because of its hierarchy of officers, the mag-
nificence of its temples, the unquestioned acceptance of its
authority by all people of whatever social class. And so it was
that Holy Week was not for him what it was to many, a time
of holiday, but a sacred fast and a deeper dedication to God.

During the Easter vacation he went to the Monastery of San
Francisco to live in consecrated quarters those eight mystic,
tragic days of Passion Week. Not for any selfish pleasure or
advantage would he have thought even of setting foot outside
the monastery grounds. Servants prepared and brought meals
to him. For these eight days, which have a special indulgence
from the Church in favour of those who observe them faithfully, he dedicated himself to a minute examination of his
conscience. He wearied his mind in the task of remembering
all the sins which in the course of the year he had committed.
As the heavy load of his guilt seemed to increase day by day,
he looked forward longingly to the time when his Confession
might be made, absolution be granted and, his sins forgiven,
he might partake of Holy Communion.

Strangely, even here in these sacred precincts where he came
to purify himself, his heart was distressed and troubled. There

were not lacking among seemingly devout worshippers who frequented the monastery ground and the pilgrims who came from a distance, those who would slip into the monks' cells, and rob them of their candy, cigars, and wine. At night, when the monks seemed to be sleeping or the gardener was perhaps off on his own errands, some would climb the walls of the orchard to steal fruit. Losses of money and other objects of value were reported. To reconcile such conduct with their spiritual exercises was an enigma too great for his young heart and mind.

But there were many beautiful hours which lifted his soul into a veritable rapture of adoration. At seven o'clock each evening everyone in the monastery would bring a lighted candle, and together they would march about the church, shadowy figures seeming to crouch behind the great pillars, and the images shifting their positions wearily. This was "The Way of the Cross" (*Via Crucis*). At regular intervals about the church building, beginning at one end of the great altar and continuing back and around the chapel until the altar was reached once more, were various scenes depicting Christ on the way to Calvary. Sad music breathed from the organ— sometimes the *misereres* were chanted by groups of priests until one's heart seemed breaking with the fearful tragedy of the "Via Dolorosa".

Good Friday was the climax of this period of devotion. From twelve o'clock to three in the afternoon the priests harangued the crowded church on the Seven Words from the Cross. Their emotions having been raised to the highest pitch, many weeping, some hysterical, Christ having died, the procession of the Holy Sepulchre would form and the body of Christ as taken from the cross would be borne in a coffin before the marching throng, all of whom carried tapers lighted at the candelabra in the church. Not only would the entire population of the town be there, dressed in black suits of mourning, for the purchase of which they had perhaps saved for an entire year, but the countryside round about would send in its throngs, and the Indians from the mountains might also be seen. By perhaps six o'clock the mournful march would be ended and the Holy Sepulchre procession returned to the church. With this ceremony Holy Week ended, save for the wild disorders of "The Saturday of Glory" (*El Sabado de*

Gloria), the following day, when Judas would be burned in effigy after his body had been kicked and hooted down the streets to an accompaniment of firecrackers and endless din. By Sunday morning many a head would be aching from alcoholic indulgence. Easter was over when Christ was dead and Judas punished, for in the Roman Church of the southland no living Christ is known or celebrated, save He who appears in a wafer upon the altars of the Church.

When Walter Manuel Montano, however, had finished these religious exercises it must be stated that the sacred devotions had produced in him a certain emotional satisfaction, a spiritual relief. He felt as though in truth he had been freed from the burden of his sins. But these emotional releases did not last long—they were scarcely more than fatuous will-o'-the-wisps which blinked out as they were born, sentiments which evaporated in the moment of experiencing them. Once he had left the monastery, the church, the ceremonies, the confession, the communion, the company of priests and prelates, the sound of solemn music, the hypnotic blaze of dancing candles, he was left without strength to continue in the path of right; he was left without spiritual power to fight against evil in himself or his environment, or to live the good life. No dyke had been built against the sea of wickedness about him or the waves of his own natural evil inclinations which beat upon his soul and tore down the tinselled trappings of an exterior religion. Not only was he left without equilibrium in the midst of a corrupt and sense-drunk world, but because he was sincere and thoughtful he was troubled by what he had observed in the conduct of his companions in those hours of holy retirement.

Thus, almost insensibly, and at an early age, childhood was dropping from him and he had begun to seek the *why* of things and to meditate, as young or old philosophers will, upon the life around him.

"Yes, he is a devout boy, a really very religious boy, indeed," said Father Ledezma, his uncle, rubbing one pudgy hand with the other. "Perhaps he, too, may be a priest, a bishop even, or well—who knows? For he is very young. To govern spiritually," added the old priest cryptically, nodding his head knowingly, "is still to govern."

"I have no fears for that boy," said Dr. German Guillen

Montano. "Desiderio, my older boy—he has left home to become a doctor; he was too violent. And Antonio has also left home—who knows where he is, poor lad! He could not get along with his stepmother; he was too old for that and too young for the world. But Walter Manuel—yes, he is a student, a little too religious now, perhaps, but he will soon be cured of that. He shall take my place as a scholar and leader of education. My work in establishing and carrying forward the rural schools shall some day be his." He crossed himself in appreciation of these favours from heaven.

But all was not to go so smoothly for the young man. One day not far from the beautiful home of the Montanos he was witness to a scurrilous attack by the sacristan of the near-by chapel on one of the parishioners. Leaving words to less warm souls, the sacristan came to blows from which the victim had to defend himself. With other spectators and the two principals in the roadside brawl, Walter Manuel was taken to the police station, where he declared informally the guilt of the sacristan and was told to report back later at the time of the trial.

The local priest at once began a house-to-house campaign in the neighbourhood and, to prove the innocence of the sacristan, obliged various persons to prepare to act as witnesses, even though they had not seen the fight. He visited Walter Manuel and insisted that he, too, should declare the guilty man's innocence.

"But I cannot do so, Father," declared the boy. "The sacristan attacked the other man vilely. He was only defending himself. He is innocent. The sacristan is guilty."

"You are condemned to hell," said the priest decisively, "unless you help establish the innocence of the sacristan."

So obstinate was Walter Manuel that parental authority had to be invoked in forcing the boy to testify as desired. The father knew nothing of the incident, but he declared, "The priest is right, of course. You must obey him." There was nothing else to do. He was to learn later that priests are always right and must always be obeyed.

When, a few days later, at the time of the trial he was placed upon the witness stand and the judge asked, "Do you swear in the name of God and the holy Catholic religion to tell the truth?" After answering in the affirmative, in obedience to his father and the parish priest, he accused the

c

innocent man and, as did all the other witnesses, declared the guilty sacristan free of all blame. When the trial was ended, the innocent man was sentenced to a term in jail and ordered to pay the sacristan an indemnity for the injuries which he had received. So do men learn to fear the power of the Catholic Church in Latin America. The dictum, "The king can do no evil", has been taken over by a ubiquitous institution whose ministers can enforce its will, and men find that it is easier to work with the Church than to oppose it.

But such close proximity to falsehood, such forced participation in perjury, was a serious thing for a young man who took his religion seriously and who as a result sought the truth. Here were unholy results. Did they spring from a holy religion as their cause? He felt a religious coldness stealing over him. Worship became not only uninteresting but even threatened to become loathsome to him. As he hated himself for his cowardice and the lies he had spoken to injure an innocent man, much more he hated the Church which had forced him to commit such a crime. But, more than that, to feel himself bound by the Church, held in a vice-like grip, directly governed by it, and when that failed to find that all of life, his own father even, could instantly become a tool of the Church for controlling his life, filled him with a feeling of futile frenzy. It was at the procession of the Holy Sepulchre on Good Friday the next year that his eyes were opened.

On this day as he was marching with the multitude in conformity to what being a "good Catholic" required, he began to study the faces of the men and women about him. "What!" thought he. "Their shameful lives would be a reproach to any cause, and yet there they are walking with downcast eyes and pious mien! And these are the Church's devotees!" He saw there young men and women who had tempted him to evil. None seemed more religious than they. The band was playing a funeral dirge. It seemed most fitting. Something was dying within him. Faith in the Church was dying. Faith in God was dying. He felt in his very soul what has turned millions away from the Catholic Church in Latin America, or at least changed them from devotees to questioning, cynical sceptics. He felt sweeping over him an overpowering revulsion against all things religious. Still he walked with downcast eyes and funereal pace back to the door of the church where the dead body of the Christ was carried inside and placed before the altar. As for him, not only Christ but all religion was dead.

But, again following the genius of his people, he discovered that if there be no truth in religion still there may be found personal utility in it. He could see that it was useful to the priests—they lived by it. It was useful to the politicians and governors of the land, for through it they controlled the lives and destinies of their subjects. Perhaps even he, Walter Manuel Montano, might find that religion could be made to serve his purposes. And such indeed was the case.

Former restraints were thrown off and more worldly minded companions cultivated. He began obtaining his father's money secretly and spending it on unworthy objects. More than once at night after the gates of the estate were locked he would swing over the wall where the pacay tree grew and, in the company of college friends, leave town for a few days of youthful frolic. When, like the prodigal son, his money was gone, and he desired to return to the parental roof-tree, religion became a faithful ally. Walter Manuel would write home, stating that he regretted having committed sin, that he had been overcome with remorse, had confessed to a priest, and for the doing of penance had received absolution. It worked like a charm. If God through His servants had pardoned the boy's sin, that placed him beyond the punishment of his father. The invitation to return was never refused. Yes, religion did have values—if one knew how to make the most of it.

On a certain occasion, he having committed a very grave fault in his home, his father punished him severely and obliged him to go to the parish priest to confess. He did not dare to disobey, but as he had not prepared himself and could not easily remember all his sins the priest began to ask him a series of questions to awaken his memory. He felt a strange horror coming over him. Later he was to learn that the priest was as much a victim of the institution he served as was the parishioner. While Walter Manuel had committed many wild pranks common to youth, he had not even known that such horrible perversions as the questions of his confessor revealed existed in human life—certainly not that he should have been thought guilty of them. He felt his moral nature weakened, twisted, sullied. He felt the fountains of his being muddied.

Later he could not shut out the terrible things which such questioning had suggested to his mind.

However, he remained the religionist *par excellence*. The more he hated and despised it, the greater was his conformity in all that pleased the Church or his friends. But his offering was that of proud, disdainful Cain. However, this could be only an episode in a character as strong as his. Sooner or later he must either cast off this cloak of hypocrisy he now wore and boldly declare his intellectual and spiritual independence of the Church, or find reality in a genuine experience of God.

That his spiritual failure was to live on in the life of Bolivia, cursing and blighting others in the years to come, he could not then know.

CHAPTER FOUR

SATAN'S COLPORTEUR

WALTER MANUEL MONTANO was fifteen years of age now. The discipline of the home had yielded to the discipline of the school. But, for him, there must be some shorter route than this which led to glory. Others had found it; so would he. Here on this southern continent, with the history of *coups d'état* and dictators all about him, with a sense of the wrong which had been done his land by Chile, there was to power, fame, and wealth one shortest way of all. "Father," he said one night after dinner, "I want to be a soldier."

"A soldier!" his father exclaimed in astonishment. "Well, a general, perhaps. For *that* there are military colleges."

"Yes, that is it. I will be a general. The examinations will open soon for the military college at La Paz. May I take them, Father?"

The father smiled to himself. He knew what those examinations were, designed to eliminate the horde of applicants who would gladly wear the epaulettes of a general. Out of a hundred who tried rarely were as many as fifteen accepted. But then it would be good experience for the boy—it would knock out of him some of that haughty cocksureness which he was beginning to display; settle him down a bit; keep him in at nights; a touch of failure would be good for him, especially if his father wished it so. "Yes," said the older man, as though he were weighing a question thoroughly, "you have my permission to take the coming examinations."

When, a few weeks later, the examinations had been concluded, a commission from the Military College of La Paz came to escort the young applicant to his new post as a student of the Government. It cost Dr. German Guillen Montano a good sum of money to have the application of his fifteen-year-old son annulled.

But what, after all, should he be or do? There was a question still unsettled. His success in passing the entry examination to the military college had increased the father's respect for him. He was precocious intellectually. Outwardly he was more religious than ever. In fact, his interest in religion had seemed to increase apace with his escapades.

Religion in Latin America, as in ancient Gaul, may be divided into three parts. There is the Roman Catholic Church, with its endless hordes of nuncios, archbishops, nuns,, pertaining to a bewildering array of separate orders such as the Jesuits, Franciscans, Dominicans, Mercedarios, Corazonists, Carmelites, Passionists, forming an ecclesiastical hierarchy, a religious ruling class, with an army of dependents whose living and continued influence depend upon the worship of the "God-of-things-as-they-are". Then there is an ever-growing company of intellectuals recruited from the student classes whose revolt at what they have seen pass for Christianity has driven them not only into frank, and sometimes, violent criticism of the Church, but into atheism. And between these two extremes may be found the women and children who appreciate the beauty of the churches, the richness of the ceremonies, the dogmatic authority of the priests, and who fear their power. As for the men in this latter group, for the most part they find it more convenient to compromise conscience, mind, and religion; and so while giving nominal support can be depended upon to appear only four times at the church—to be christened, to be confirmed, to be married, and to be buried. And then on the periphery of South American life is the sea of Indians whose life is still largely guided by their ancient gods, though they may call them by Christian names.

While Walter Manuel found that religion could be made to serve his own purpose, it was a cheap and easy compromise which could not long endure. He could not, would not, for long, drift with the tide. He could not long endure to have as an answer to the deepest quest of the human heart only hypocritical form and mere superstition. Thought and study demanded of him a philosophy of life which had enough vitality to stand the strain of scientific method. If there were a God he must at last find Him and serve Him. If there were none the fierce passion of his mind must inevitably tear down the false mask of religion and give to him that dangerous freedom which so largely has come to modern man.

Hypocrisy in his own life led him to suspect hypocrisy in others. If he were using the Church as a means to his own ends, and succeeding admirably as a religionist without any religion, the question naturally insinuated itself in his mind as to whether the leaders in the Church were not doing the same. He could see clearly, though the full force of this insight was hidden from him for a time, that the priest, instead of making religion a way of life, made it a way of living. At times he revolted at the whole system, and inwardly hated the Church and its priests, but the social pressure of family and friends and habit, instilled from his infancy, maintained in him an admirable conformity. He hated himself for his grovelling, lying hypocrisy, and he began to hate even more the Church which encouraged it, approved it, rewarded it. The alternative to his mode of life, bound as he was to the present order by the social caste of a ruling clan, was so unthinkable that only a tremendous spiritual and moral crisis could have led him to take it.

One day as this questioning youth and some of his companions came down the flagstone walk of the Cochabamba College on to the street, a Catholic priest was standing at the corner talking to a group of boys. It could be seen that he was explaining something to his listeners which greatly interested him and them. Perhaps he had imbibed a little too freely of the goodly liquors which church life provided in such abundance, or again it may have been that out of his evil heart was pouring forth, uncensored, that which was his life.

The priest's talk centred about the girls' school which could be seen standing at no great distance from the men's building. His obscenities need not be reported here. At times he seemed to think his sallies humorous and laughed uproariously at them himself, looking about occasionally to make sure that no lady passer-by was near. In the group there were no doubt those who enjoyed his remarks. As for Walter Manuel, when he first came up he did not understand what was taking place. As the full force of the horrible suggestions began to dawn upon him he felt a horror, then a fury. He was one who had an inherent sense of nobility which had kept him from many of the grosser practices around him. The mere mention of evil things might not have shocked him, but this was God's messenger speaking. Not only was it what the man said, as he stood there grimacing and gesticulating, which troubled him, but this man was a symbol of that religion which pretended to be the arbiter of morals and the guide to heaven; a religion which had frightened him with tales of hell to make him its slave; which had forced him to lie when its interests were at stake; that demanded of him obeisance in the form of penance which it imposed in judgment upon his conduct; and now the representative of that religion stood on the corner and poured into his ear the filthy, lecherous plans of a *roué*.

He was through with it all. A great volcano burst within his soul. He would believe their lies no longer, nor would he pretend to do them reverence for his own advantage. From this hour he could be counted on as an enemy of the Church. He would be an atheist. Whatever the cost, he became an atheist in that very moment. He would form an atheist club. He would fight this thing called religion with all his strength. As for this swine on the corner, he could have killed him at the moment. Without waiting for the priestly blessing he and his companions strode on down the street. The sort of revolution which recently has been twisting governments off their foundations had occurred—so far as he was concerned.

The next day Walter Manuel went to the largest bookstore in Cochabamba. "I want a book against God," he demanded boldly.

"You want what?" asked the astonished clerk.

"A book against God!" he repeated.

"*Dios mio.* Are you joking?" asked the man in amazement.

"No, here is my money," said the wistful young atheist.

The clerk hunted long and assiduously, dug around on back shelves, and finally emerged with a volume. "This one is *Christ Never Existed*. It is all that I can find," he said apologetically.

"That will do," was his reply. "How much is it?"

When the volume had been purchased the boy and the clerk went into consultation as to the best means of securing other atheist literature. After consulting catalogues and studying the matter it was decided to send an order to La Paz, the capital of Bolivia.

As throughout all Latin America where atheism is flourishing side by side with the most abject superstition, the ground had already been prepared in the minds of a considerable number of younger men for this revolt against God. Probably eighty per cent. of nominal Roman Catholics in South

America regret the abuses in their Church and long for reform providing it does not come through the Protestants. As the boys discussed matters over the pages of this volume which claimed to prove their position and make the denial of deity intellectually respectable, it was decided to form an organization to give greater strength to their position, and in that moment the "Students' Atheist Association" was formed. It still exists. It has turned out a yearly alumni which has been fostering atheism throughout South America. It has been spiritual tragedy in many a life. Dr. Alberto Cornejo, a brilliant lawyer and active atheist, is a product of this group, as is Dr. Carlos Walter Urquidi, a lawyer of international repute in South America, recently honoured by appointment to a commission of seven to draw up a new constitution for Bolivia. The work of this group of religious rebels was successful, a great deal too successful, and its activities today in Bolivia have become a serious obstacle to the advancement of the gospel—but that is a part of the story yet to be told.

The college authorities grew alarmed at the rapid growth of atheism, and as a means of checking its advance a Franciscan father was asked to establish a course of religion at the Bolivian National College of Cochabamba. Attendance was compulsory. Therefore the class was detested by all. As for Walter Manuel, he became the butt for many campus jokes about atheists who take college courses in religion.

There was only one way to retain a shred of manly independence in such circumstances—to torment the instructor. He was caught red-handed one day. The professor at once proceeded to enter failure in his classbook, which meant the loss of a year's work to the younger man. But later an attempt to steal and destroy the offending record was successful. He also purchased and distributed among the students large quantities of atheistic literature.

Now instead of kneeling before the priests when he met them in the street and asking for the picture of some saint, or requesting, "Father, bless me!" he would make fun wherever he dared to, calling out unpleasant names, or hiding behind trees and shrubs and throwing stones their way. To the little stamp saints which once had been worshipped so devoutly vulgar additions were made. Christ Himself became the object of horrible blasphemies. Church doors were written upon clandestinely. "Down with the priests!" was the cry. Judging by its fruits, atheism is a very poor substitute for Romanism.

But still, so deeply religious is the human heart, Walter Manuel could not leave God alone nor find the way to live without Him. One day as he sat in his study in his father's beautiful home a question suddenly spoke itself to his mind as though another were present with him. "*Why* are you an atheist?" asked the Voice.

The question startled him. For his life he could not have given a reason why. He knew the arguments which had been learned and passed on to others. He knew the hate and scorn with which he viewed what had been presented to him as religion. But, after all, did he *know* that there was no God? Outside his window, festooned with flower-laden wreaths of bougainvillia, above the tops of the flowering tropical trees, buttressed by grey-brown, purple-blue mountains of towering granite, he might have seen the eternal snows of the Upper Andean peaks. But within the unlighted caverns of his being a storm was raging.

"Why *are* you an atheist?" Well, after all, was he an atheist? He had hated sham, he had sickened at the hypocritical blasphemy he had seen in the lives of priests and devotees. But was not this violent reaction the result of a belief in a God of holiness, purity, and love? Was not his very atheism an expression of unguided loyalty to such a God? Perhaps, after all, his hatred of religion was only true religion perverted. Perhaps his atheism was only another declaration of the fact that "the soul is made for God, and cannot rest until it rests in God", the blind efforts of man's mind to tear away sham, pretence, and unreality in an attempt to find a personal experience of God.

"Why are *you* an atheist?" If one needed to be sure of the existence of God to worship Him one certainly needed to be just as sure there was no God before ignoring Him. After all, mere prejudice, mere revulsion at abuses could not well furnish a philosophy by which to live. To build on that was certainly to lay foundations on sand and not on rock. How was one to face the great eternities of God with nothing more sure than this? He laughed at himself. Here he was thinking and reasoning like one of the priests he professed to despise. Who knew whether there was any life after death? Even

Solomon asked, "Who knoweth the spirit of man that goeth upward, and the spirit of the beast that goeth downward to the earth?" And as for God, why should he be thinking of Him at all?

"Face it!" persisted the Voice. "Can you tell why, after all, you are an atheist? Can you prove that there positively is no God? Can you, without God, understand this material world of yours with all its infinite order and unity, its purpose and design? Can you unravel the mystery of organic life even in the simplest creature, let alone the vaulting spirit of man? Is your failure to find and know God sufficient proof that there is no God? Perhaps you have not taken the proper means of finding Him. Perhaps you have stopped short of discovery, as a miner who seeks for gold and, having spent much time and strength, quits his quest just when fortune is near at hand. Like him you have only the dirt and sand and rock of materialism while you might be enjoying spiritual wealth. Face it! Give an answer which will stand throughout eternity. Why are you an atheist?"

"I cannot answer that," replied the young man to himself. "I cannot prove that there is no God. To say that the world made itself—that is folly. To say that it always was is to make it God. Perhaps I have not gone far enough in religion to find Him. Because a few priests were evil and a few worshippers immoral—that is not to prove that there is no God. If I were to become a priest myself, perform the offices of the Church with a pure heart; if I were to dedicate myself in penances and fasts and mighty vigils, spend long hours in prayer before the altars of the Church; if I were to read only the books of those who knew Him in centuries past, then no doubt I would find Him. To be an atheist, of course, is to be nothing."

Walter Manuel Montano knew of but one religion, for the message of Protestant missions in South America rarely reached the educated classes. God had, so far as he knew, but one means of expressing Himself through revelation other than the book of nature, and that was the Apostolic Roman Catholic Church. God would be found there or not at all. Well, for one, he would find Him. His present life was intolerable. He would return to the Church. He would dedicate his life to the service of God and religion. He himself would become a priest!

Someone may ask, "If the Voice spoke to Walter Manuel Montano at all, why was he not now guided into fuller light and truth?"

And the only answer one can give is the story of the years which lay ahead.

CHAPTER FIVE

A RENEGADE ATHEIST

Now that Walter Manuel had decided to become a priest the next step was to secure his father's approval.

A few days after the momentous decision Walter Manuel walked back from his study at the rear of the large home to his father's spacious library. As he looked around him at the shelves of books, the profusion of antique carvings, the archæalogical findings, the rich rugs on the floor, all indicating wealth and leisure, it would have been impossible for him to realize that soon a turn of the wheel of political fortune would thrust the older man into the chill damp of a prison cell, subject him to be beaten, naked, until his flesh should cringe from the stinging blows—that this rich home would be left deserted, while his father would find refuge, alone, in cheap lodgings, to hide from his enemies. But today he was the "Kaiser" in the steel-grey prime of life.

As the would-be priest entered the richly furnished room his father was absorbed in a large volume. He waited a few moments, hesitating to disturb him, then finally ventured, "Good afternoon, Father. May I talk with you?"

"Yes, yes, my son," replied the older man mechanically, never looking up from his reading. "How are you today?"

"But, Father, I have something important to say to you. You must help me plan and decide."

"Yes, yes, my son. How are you?"

"But, Father, I want to become a priest!"

Dr. German Guillen Montano laid down the volume upon which he had been meditating, removed his glasses, and looked steadily and searchingly at his son as though to ascertain either his sanity or his seriousness. Was this some jest, perhaps, or a threat by which he hoped to obtain money or favour? He could see only earnest youth in quest.

"A priest?" he answered in amazement. "Whatever put such a thought into your head, my son?"

As best he could the young man told the story.

"Hum-m-m-m!" replied the older man when his son had

45

finished, not quite sure just what course to take. "You at least could never be a common priest—I could not permit that. You might, however, if you insist on this, become a monk."

So most of the afternoon was spent in discussing this momentous decision. To the father it was a revelation of the spiritual depth of his son. To Walter Manuel came the discovery of a father who really seemed to care concerning his future. Together they talked of life and destiny, pondered the mystery and meaning of divine revelation through the Church, and discussed the difficulties and privations of a monk's life.

If the boy's father had thought that these might deter his son from the priesthood he was disappointed. For Walter Manuel it meant that he could never marry nor have a home of his own. As he thought of his stepmother it seemed to him that this would involve no sacrifice. He was too young to know that a home and a family of children of one's own can prove life's greatest joy. He could see clearly that the austerities of a monk's life would demand of him a discipline about which he knew nothing. But still, for him, the overpowering passion of knowing God was what counted most.

A few mornings later his father called Walter Manuel on to the terrace overlooking the beautiful garden of tropical plants and shrubs. Above the wall which enclosed the *patio* loomed the ever-present, awesome heights of the Andes, today glistening diamond-white against the blue-black depths of the sky like witnesses to the majesty and power of the Creator. As the young man seated himself at the rustic reading table the older man asked, "Are you still determined to be a monk?"

"Yes, surely," answered the young candidate.

"How would you like to be a Franciscan?" asked his father.

Walter Manuel thought of the hospice of the Franciscans in Cochabamba. Their life seemed so humdrum. He had rather despised them in the past. "No," answered the young man, "I would rather be something else."

His father had a pile of magazines and catalogues describing the numerous orders of the Catholic Church. As they studied the various monasteries and discussed their relative merits, Walter Manuel's interest was gradually attracted to that of the Dominican Friars. It was the wealthiest and most famous of them all. At the time of the founding of the order the Pope, who in that bygone day alone was permitted to preach, had, as a special honour to Santo Domingo, the founder, bestowed upon him and his monks in their fight against the Albigenses the right also to preach. Only a Dominican Friar might place "O.P." (*Ordinis Prædicatorum*) after his name, signifying Preaching Order. Not only was preaching the prerogative of the Dominicans, but they were also required to spend eight hours a day in study until the day of their death, and their traditions told of many great scholars who graced their history. They had also been honoured by having the Inquisition entrusted to them. Their shield carried three words, "Praise, Bless, Preach" (*Laudare, Benedicere, Prædicare*), which expressed their purposes. Even the Pope exercised comparatively little control over them, as they had their own spiritual head in Rome.

At Lima, Peru, was one of the richest and most aristocratic monasteries of the Dominican Order in all Latin America. To be admitted there would be in keeping with the social prestige of the family. The robes were also most attractive—white with a great black cape of many yards of cloth, much like that worn by royalty in former days. The Dominican monks were different men from the priests he had known around Cochabamba. Walter Manuel could tell that from their pictures and the stories of the order. These men evidently knew God. God was pleased to reveal Himself to them. Together father and son decided the momentous question—he would be a Dominican monk—if they would accept him.

In the Montano family various emotions prevailed. To the father it meant the loss of a son but the saving of the family name. He had heard rumours of his son's activities among the members of the Students' Atheist Association. He thought of it only as youthful folly which had no real meaning for the boy's life, and yet the possibility of his son's becoming an atheist agitator was a sinister shadow upon the older man's life. The stepmother, however, was to be relieved of a problem which had many times caused friction in the home. In the servants' quarters it was viewed as nothing less than an irreparable loss, but as unquestioning adherents of the Church they could not but rejoice in the thought of the young man whom they all loved becoming a monk.

Rumours spread around the Alameda, where the members

of the Students' Atheist Association met on park benches. There had been a defection from their ranks. Their leader and founder had decided to become a priest—a monk, even. It was incredible, impossible! It must be some caprice of his youth. He would never go to Lima. It was a trick to buy some new privilege of which they knew nothing. He would soon be back among them. But as the years ahead were to prove, the Students' Atheist Association was now so well established that it could, if need be, function without him.

How strange are the deep currents of life on which, sometimes unconsciously, we find ourselves borne along. Blasphemous atheism was eating into the religious and moral life of Cochabamba because a youth's reason revolted at the hypocrisies and immoralities which he saw committed in the name of Christ by the leaders of the Church. But one day a Voice spoke in his consciousness and impulses came from some hidden source which carried him from a life of revolt to the cloisters of the Dominican Friars. What he came to know of monastery life is part of the story yet untold.

CHAPTER SIX

THE DEATH OF WALTER MANUEL MONTANO

SOON the necessary formalities of entry into the monastery*
had been completed and word came of his acceptance.

Despite the first flush of joy there was also sadness. There
was something so final about becoming a monk. He would be
bidding farewell to father and family for ever. His past liberties
were ended. For him there could be no turning back. Political
ambitions, fanned by his Uncle Eliodoro Villazon, former
President of Bolivia, were for ever ended. He was deciding
the most momentous question of his life "sight unseen", for
what, after all, did he or the family know of the actual experiences which awaited him?

On February 9th, 1920, at the age of seventeen years, the
journey began. His father held him longer than usual in the
customary embrace. Then as the train pulled out he stood on
the rear platform waving to friends and family until they faded
into the distance and, as the train rounded a curve, the town
itself was swallowed up in the folds of the rolling hills.

For a considerable time he could still see the great trees
which stood guard above his home, which, beautiful as a poet's
dream in the warm morning sunshine, its gardened terraces
crowded with flowering shrubs and fronded palms, appeared
like some modern hanging gardens, with its white-walled *patios*
and red-tiled roofs radiant against the purple background of
the Andes. But no more would he join in celebrating the Feast
of Santa Ana; no more sit carefree in the evening while the
band played and soft-voiced Indian maids served the native
drinks and dishes of spiced chicken; no more follow the in-
tricate steps of the handkerchief dance, with the bright-eyed
señoritas luring yet always escaping one. All this was gone
for ever. Henceforth he must be content with the mysteries of
the monastery.

At La Paz, the capital of Bolivia, from whose bookstores
only a short time before his atheistic literature was being
shipped, a friend of the family who acted as his companion

---

* Convento Maximo del Santisimo Rosario de Lima, Peru.

delivered him into the hands of a Dominican monk.* This man, a famed theologian, continued religious lectures for two weeks, during which time Walter Manuel Montano was placed in the monastery Conventa de los Salecianos for safe keeping, lest he lose his "divine vocation". The brothers of the convent never permitted him out of their sight. A strange sadness and loneliness was besieging his heart. For years he had lived within the invisible walls of social caste, which no one may scale either from within or from without. Now he was being shut within an even smaller circle, bound by walls still more impregnable—his destiny, for this life at least, determined by others.

The Andes which Walter Manuel had always loved seemed still nearer to him here. The city was entirely surrounded by their dark heights. At dawn he saw the golden fire upon their highest crest and watched the deep blue of their shadowy depths yield to the sun's alchemy. At night he watched the grey and purple shadows creep up their ancient slopes until their snowy tops were tinted crimson, rose, and mauve, and then, as the last green and gold faded from the western sky, he saw their peaks silhouetted against the stars. In Lima he would lose that nearness. This was part of the sadness which overwhelmed him.

Walter Manuel addressed some of the Indians here in the Quechua language, which he had learned from his Indian nurse-maid, but was met with a stolid stare from the big-boned Aymaras of this region. Centuries before the Incas came, the forefathers of these Aymara Indians had been conquered by the Quechuas, but still they maintained their aboriginal tongue and their blood stream free from admixture with other races.

When, two weeks later, they journeyed towards Lake Titicaca life became more interesting to Walter Manuel. Here was a region strewn with the prehistoric remains of great mega-lithic temples and huge carved gods. Whence had they come, those immense pieces of masonry which modern machinery would be unable to move? No one knew. Even the wise men of the Inca Empire a thousand years and more ago could give no answer. One great stone god stood with three immense

* Father Cristobal Vásquez.

tears still falling from either eye as though in that bygone age he had surmised the sorrows which should come upon this land.

Their course took them across Lake Titicaca, the highest navigable body of water in the world. And yet so high did the Andes tower above it that he could scarcely convince himself that their boat was more than two miles above sea level. They passed near the famous church* where is carved above the doorway in Spanish, "Come unto Mary and she will give you rest".

At Puno, the port on the Peruvian side of the lake, Walter Manuel's interest centred in the Indian boats—*balsas*—made from seeds bound together in large rope-like masses. What thrilling, almost tragic, incidents he was to experience in the future in this little port he could not then know.

Then by rail across the furnace-like desert to the Peruvian port of Mollendo on the Pacific Ocean, where they embarked for Callao and thence by train a few miles to the great metropolis of Lima.

In the railway station in Lima, Walter Manuel called a porter to carry his grips and valises. "No, you carry them," ordered the monk who had charge of him.

With shame burning in his cheeks, for the first time in his life he started to carry his own belongings. The Negroes laughed to see a man whose derby hat indicated him to be of the better class carrying baggage through the streets.

They turned into the College of St. Thomas Aquinas, a two-storey building connected with the monastery, and went on through the cloisters beyond. Here Walter Manuel was formally delivered into the hands of the Superior.

When, a short time later, the young man was subjected to confession by one of the monks, he was so agitated at having been compelled to carry his own luggage that he could remember scarcely any of his sins.

Ten days were now passed in preliminary religious exercises. Excluded from association with all priests except their own Superior, Father Morales, without even the privilege of conversing with one another, Walter Manuel, with the three other candidates for the novitiate, prepared himself with

* The Church of Copacabana, where is worshipped "Nuestra Señora de Copacabana".

prayers, confessions, fasts, and the Mass for entering upon his sacred duties. He studied Thomas à Kempis' *Imitation of Christ*, Fray Luis de Granada's *Guide to Sinners*, and enormous tomes giving the stories of the heroic sacrifices of those who lived for the Church, of the death of her martyrs, and vivid descriptions of hell which left him trembling with fear.

Having completed his preparations, on March 25th, Solemn Feast Day of the Virgin Mary, Walter Manuel Montano and his three companions were taken to the traditional altar inside the monastery, unseen save by the monks, and here, during an impressive ceremony, his outer garments were removed, signifying the laying aside of his former life, and the black-and-white habit of a Dominican friar was blessed and placed upon him. Then he lay down in front of the altar while a burial ceremony was read over him. Thus did he die to the world, to live in the service of the Church. Then, kneeling, he repeated the vow, "I, Walter Manuel Montano, promise to observe the vows of chastity, poverty, and obedience."

Later, as the bells tolled and the organ shook the building with its thunderous tones, they marched to the great altar of the Church of Santo Domingo, where again they were solemnly and publicly consecrated to the new life of a novitiate.

He thrilled to the Superior's sermon: "Deny yourself"— divest yourself of your own will, liberty, humanity, annihilate personality, destroy your own character, surrender to the will of your superiors, whether just or unjust; "Take up your cross" —practise penances, privations, mortification of the body, wear sackcloth, use the scourge, fasting, silence; "Follow me" —enter the monastery, live behind its walls, flee from society, leave the light of day. He listened with a sort of ecstasy to think that he had become as one of the Apostles in leaving all to follow the Christ.

Thus he and his three fellow novitiates came into newness of life. They were then led away to their cells, where, separated even from the other priests, they were to live alone their year of trial. Not only did they have their own cells but a separate living-room and chapel.

Walter Manuel Montano's name was changed to Fray Luis, after his patron saint, Luis Beltran, whose penance, preaching ability, and missionary zeal he earnestly desired to imitate.

The orbit of his life had now been fixed for ever—prayers, confessions, masses, study, chanting—fixed for ever.

A letter from his father read, "My son, whom I worship, thou hast died to this miserable and cursed world."

Yes, Walter Manuel Montano no longer existed. He had died upon the altars of the Church.

CHAPTER SEVEN

THE LIFE OF FRAY LUIS

THE life of Fray Luis had begun. His world was a much smaller one than he had ever known before. It consisted only of the living quarters and chapel of the novitiate. Besides the Superior of the novitiates, Friar Morales, he had contact with none of the other monks except during the three daily prayer periods in the choir, morning, afternoon, and evening. When their devotions were chanted a single session might require two hours.

In addition the novitiates had their own special prayers from another prayer book lasting about half an hour preceding breakfast, dinner, and time for retirement. But these exercises did not take the place of their own private devotions, which required from thirty minutes to an hour each day of repeating the Lord's Prayer and counting the beads of the rosary. There were also periods when they must lie down and concentrate their thought upon the Passion of Christ and the sufferings of the Virgin Mary. Lest mealtimes should prove a snare and their minds stray from religious themes to worldly affairs, one of the friars would read portions of the Bible in Latin, thus covering that sacred book in the course of the year. There were many special days, such as Friday for the Sacred Heart of Jesus and Saturday for devotions to the Virgin Mary, which consumed other hours. The world which he had once known seemed very far away indeed. If his world were smaller it was certainly a more intense one than he had ever known before.

But Fray Luis felt that he was at last finding reality. There was no room for question. Under the pressure of long hours of study the doctrine and dogma of the Church were steadily welding themselves into a magnificent structure of thought, a veritable city of God, which was matched by the outward power and splendour of the great institution which, in His stead, ruled on earth. As far as he was then able to discern, deception and error and despicable twisting of truth into falsehood were at an end. Here in the discipline of a novitiate's life was no ignorant immorality parading itself as a cure for souls.

That which he had known and at which he had revolted in Cochabamba was some strange excrescence on the body of Christ. He was living now in a world which was real, eternal—God's world. While he had not yet come to a personal knowledge of God, nevertheless Fray Luis was confident that he was drawing nearer to that revelation—he might expect at any time that the vision would break forth upon him.

From that outside world which seemed so far away, whose preoccupations were already beginning to seem some dreamed-of fever, whose struggles, disappointments, and achievements began to appear some strange fantasy, there came to him only an occasional letter, always opened, read, and censored by the Superior lest something which might lessen his devotion or distract his mind might reach him. Letters which he addressed to friends in that far-away unreal world must also pass through the hands of the Superior to avoid any untoward expression which might cast a reflection on life within the monastery. He was forbidden even to think upon the death of his most intimate friend or that of a relative. He could not have so much as a photograph of his own mother. In his room was a picture of the Virgin of the Rosary—his spiritual Mother, of Santo Domingo—his spiritual father; a crucifix—his devotion.

At times some phrase in his father's letter or some chance message of a friend who had not forgotten would awaken memories which stung and burned. He would see his home in all its glory of eternal springtime, feel once more the spell of the lofty snow-crowned Andes ever watching above him, remember the hoped-for career which he had tossed aside. There were times when the tears would flood his eyes as he recalled the insufferable desperation which had swept over him as the final embrace was being given him by his father and he had bid farewell to all that had ever been for him a home.

Day by day his devotion to the Virgin Mary was increasing. She listened to his every passing sorrow, forgave his sins, was always smiling down upon him benignly—never chided him. He had never known a woman like that since those long-ago days when at three years of age his mother had wearily lain down to sleep the last long sleep of earth. He loved the Virgin as he felt he would have loved his mother had she lived.

One night he dreamed that Santo Domingo, Founder of the

Order, appeared and commanded him to use on his flesh a rough, leather instrument (*Lao Disciplinas*) made of knotted thongs with pieces of steel in the end tied to a short handle, with which one may scourge his own back or that of another to produce spiritual growth. After following the mystic instructions of his nocturnal visitor until his back was a mass of sores he confessed it to one of his fathers. This man ordered him to pay no attention to his dreams. Perhaps the career of a devotee such as has lifted some into the category of the saintly heroes of the Church was thus ended.

One day as the Superior passed the group of novitiates he struck Fray Luis full upon the chest and said, "Do you know why I like you? Because you are serious and never laughing, as other novitiates."

Yes, Walter Manuel Montano had indeed died. Fray Luis was beginning to live—at least it seemed like living now. As with many another religionist, it had been well for him if Fray Luis had always remained a novitiate. Organized religion in Latin America—and elsewhere—so often acquires characteristics so unlike Christ that the Master is lost among His minions, and the better one knows it the less he knows its Founder.

If the Virgin brought solace she could also produce a storm to threaten his new world.

CHAPTER EIGHT

A DECEPTIVE VIRGIN

At the end of the first year Fray Luis was one of the three who passed the examinations and became eligible for reception into the Simple Profession.

Again there were ten days of most rigorous spiritual preparation, after which he repeated his vows of chastity, poverty, and obedience, for a further period of three years. At this time he was ordered to sign a formal renunciation of all right, title, and interest in any property whatsoever which he did now or ever should possess, all of which was granted to the Dominican Order, and the paper sealed before a notary.

The members of the Simple Profession were removed to cells about fourteen by eighteen feet in size, where, aside from the objects of worship, there were to be found only a bed, lavatory, clothes' closet, book-shelves, and writing-table.

As in the novitiate, so now in the Simple Profession, this group had a separate chapel of their own. While they had more liberty than formerly, still they did not have the opportunity of free intercourse with the other friars. Simple pleasures, however, began for them. Fray Luis raised ducks and chickens. In this way the loneliness became a little more bearable. Some raised dogs, doves, and various other pets—so fundamental to our very existence it seems is the necessity of the society of others who are dependent upon us.

The liberalism of some of his teachers disturbed the orthodoxy of Fray Luis at times. When told of a chapel in the United States of America where the Catholics worshipped in the morning and the Protestants at night, how could he reconcile the thought that one group was worshipping God in the morning, and the other group worshipping the devil at night? But asking questions was not encouraged, as he well knew.

One day as Father Pandigozo was teaching the doctrine of Peter as the rock on which the true Church was built and the Pope as the successor of Peter, it occurred to Fray Luis to inquire about a discrepancy in practice which he discerned.

"How is it," he asked, "that while Christ and Peter both lived a very poor life, and had not even a place to lay their heads, that the Pope today has such immense riches and power?"

Father Pandigozo turned upon his interlocutor with savage directness. "Don't you know," he demanded, frowning fiercely, "that this is a matter of faith?" He picked up a book. "You say that this book is yellow. It seems yellow to you. But if the Church says that this book is black, then you know that it *is* black—for you that book *is* black!"

The students' own immediate Superior also instilled into them the same spirit of blind acceptance of the will and teachings of the Church. "One day," he said, "San Francisco was being assisted by a novitiate in planting onions. 'Plant that onion upside-down,' commanded San Francisco. 'No, Father, not so,' responded the student, 'for to plant it so with the top down is to work contrary to the laws of logic and of the onion.' 'Go to your home at once!' ordered San Francisco. 'You are not fit for the priesthood.'

"San Francisco then called another novitiate. 'Plant this onion upside-down,' he commanded. The novitiate, in absolute obedience, did so, and immediately there sprouted from the ground a miraculous onion plant producing large onions."

But one of his severest testings came as a result of having been appointed the awakener. As such he carried the keys to the building, and it was his duty to arise at 4.30 a.m., arouse the priests, and have the church doors open by five o'clock. As he had not yet had a look at the city of Lima he decided to make use of the opportunities which now were his. At about one o'clock in the morning, after having spent some hours in the great tower studying the outline of Lima, as he was passing down the darkened galleries along the side of the open court on his way to his cell he saw two figures standing in the shadows of the columns. They proved to be older monks of the Solemn Profession. One of them stepped towards him, and asked gruffly, "What are you doing here, Fray Luis?"

"The clock deceived me, Father," the young man answered. "I was going to call the priests." But the next morning the matter so disturbed his conscience that he told the entire affair to his Confessor. His penance for this infringement of the rules was to kiss the feet of all the friars while they were eating the evening meal, as they sat in a semi-circle with their backs to the wall, facing the Bible reader.

The discipline was indeed very hard for these young monks. The Superior meant that it should be. If there was any rebellion or self-will that later might cause a defection he desired to discover it now. The spirit of the men must be broken so far as possible so that they should for ever become faithful sons of the Order.

But the Roman Church furnished solace for its devotees. Consciously or unconsciously she provided companionship through an order of supernatural beings, humans now made saints. While Fray Luis was not conscious of this process at the time, he was later to find that women usually are devotees of the men saints and the men of the women saints. Thus does the Church take the natural force of love and the desire for the fellowship of the opposite sex, which it ostensibly seeks to extirpate, and turn it to its own uses. And later also he was to see that his relationship to the beautiful Virgin of the Rosary which hung in his room and smiled upon him the first thing in the morning and the last thing at night was very like that of an enamoured youth.

Always did the priests seek out the most beautiful pictures of the Virgin. While he had been denied a picture of his mother, still he wore pasted on the face of his watch the most bewitching face of the Virgin he was able to find. But it was more than a picture. According to the dogma of the Church it is possible for the spirit of one who has been raised to the rank of saint to be in all parts of the world at one and the same time wherever his or her picture or image is being worshipped.

Occasionally now he was visiting the country estates of the wealthy friends of the Order. He was ashamed to find that some of the friars would become so drunk that it was necessary to return them to their cells in automobiles. On one of these excursions a Father Carpio, while in a bestial state of intoxication, began to curse and insult Fray Luis in the foulest of language. He finally backed up his words by striking him deliberately in the face. Fray Luis' saintliness was not sufficient for this test. He turned and struck Father Carpio one blow which was enough to send him sprawling into the alfafa growing under the peach trees through which they were coming.

For such blasphemy, as thus having laid violent hands upon the Lord's anointed, the penalties were written in the constitution of the Order and their books of discipline. It made no difference that the injured party was drunk, was insulting, was vilely defamatory in his remarks—he was a priest of the Solemn Profession and his injury must be avenged. Fray Luis was required to lie down in the doorway of the dining-room that evening and permit the members of the chapel to walk over his prostrate body for the good of his soul and the monastery in general.

The Superior of the Simple Profession had an almost sadistic delight, it seemed, in humiliating the friars. Without reason he would many times make them kneel down before others, even strangers. They would sometimes ask, "Why do you do these things? Why should we be treated in this way?" The answer would be still further and more prolonged punishment.

During a visit to the Provincial, who had general charge of the Dominican Order in Peru, Fray Luis made a speech in which he lauded another man who had taken the Superior's place for a time, and whose kindness had made a deep impression on those of the Simple Profession. As the remarks were of necessity derogatory to the other, he was at once called by the Provincial. "You should be happy with anyone who is put over you," announced this worthy, "whether he be good or bad. It is not for you to choose what is best, but to accept all of God's will."

In heaviness of heart Fray Luis requested of the Provincial permission to leave the monastery, which at this period of the Simple Profession would have been possible. The official replied, "It can be arranged, but you will be lost and damned for ever. There can be no heaven for a man who has once begun the career of a Dominican monk and then refuses to go forward. These trials are a help to you and will cause you to grow in grace and humility."

But one day as he was walking about the grounds behind the room (the Sacrista) adjacent to the chapel where the priests put on their ornaments and arranged their costumes for the ceremonies he found a walled-in hole which he had not noticed before. Walking up to it curiously he found himself staring at an assortment of saints which had formerly been worshipped as miraculous images in the church. Some of them were badly

weathered by exposure, parts of the painted surface of their
cheeks were peeling off due to exposure to the sun, and what
remained of their clothing was bedraggled and soiled. Here
was the place of missing saints. Their final glory was but dust.
They could not even protect themselves from the elements.

"What!" philosophized Fray Luis, "have not these saints
miraculous powers? Have they not cured disease, made sterile
women bear, brought prosperity to their devotees, given yearn-
ing young ladies lovers, and brought sweethearts into the arms
of ardent youths? They have stayed plague, pestilence, and
earthquake—when did they lose their power?" Doubts so deep
and terrible assailed him that he would gladly have banished
from his mind the discovery of these ghastly remains of what
had once been objects of religious devotion and worship.

Day by day his devotion to the Virgin of the Rosary was
growing greater. Every night before going to bed he worshipped her in special prayers. On Saturdays litanies were sung
in her honour and endless praises accorded "the Daughter of
the Father, the Mother of Jesus, and the Wife of the Holy
Ghost".

In the book, *The Glory of the Rosary*, it was recorded as
solemn history that this Virgin would at times change the
colour of her face, thus expressing her anger or pleasure, de-
pending on the attentions which she received from the be-
lievers. Certainly Fray Luis had no reason to doubt a story
which was sealed by the approbation of the highest Catholic
authorities.

It was nearing the time of the national election when one
night as Fray Luis was repeating the rosary he noticed that
Mary's face was very pale, in fact, it had been growing whiter
day by day. There must be some impending calamity, or perhaps the populace were failing in their devotion. After finish-
ing prayers and while going to his room he suddenly remembered that he had left his cape in the priests' room. As he
returned to this small building again and stepped inside he
noticed an unusual light in the chapel and the sound of movement there.

At the celebration of the centenary of Peru's independence
President Augusto Leguia, a devoted supporter of the Dominican Order, had presented the Virgin with a golden crown and
sceptre of great value. It could easily be that thieves were at

work in the church. Perhaps the extreme paleness of the Virgin's face had been a warning of this.

Cautiously Fray Luis stepped into the shadows of the dimly-lighted church. For a moment he was too astonished to believe the testimony of his eyes. He saw not thieves but the devout woman who had charge of the female saints' clothes and the sacristan busily engaged putting rouge upon the cheeks of the Virgin. There was nothing for him to do. Discovery there at that hour would have led to punishment. Hastily he retired, his heart pounding with indignation. It was as though he had found someone desecrating the person of his mother.

The next day the monks took part in a very solemn service in honour of the Virgin. The church was crowded. The sacristan was preaching a sermon extolling the administration of President Leguia, and well he might, as this friend of the Dominican Order frequently sent cases of the finest champagne to the friars, showed them every possible political favour, and they in turn, through the confessional, discovered for him incipient rebellions and plots against his life. At the climax of his address the sacristan shouted, "You have seen the pallid cheeks of our Holy Mother recently. We have been asking for a sign so that we might know if our Virgin of the Rosary wished the re-election of President Leguia as president of this republic. See!" he cried, pointing towards her, "her pale cheeks are rosy once more! The Virgin has spoken. President Leguia must be re-elected in reverence, veneration, and devotion to our Most Holy Mother."

When Fray Luis entered his cell that night he studied closely the face of the Virgin which hung upon the wall. She neither blushed nor blanched, only smiled back softly, gently, winsomely as ever. Was it a hypocrite's smile? Was she unconscious of what was being done? But how could that be? If she did not know the deceptions and trickery of which she had become a part how could she know anything at all—his hours of saying prayers, for instance, when at last he felt that her eyes moved slightly in acknowledgment of his fervid devotions? She was either a willing part of the programme or the whole cult of Mary was a weird superstition. He had been taught and he had taught others that deception and trickery might be a holy means to a holy end. But it seemed different tonight. He could not so easily convince himself. If she failed him, what did he have left? How could he continue? If he lost her he would lose the only love which held him as he launched forth upon the career of a friar. But perhaps, after all, it was best to accept the teachings of the Church. More devotion, not less, was what he needed. His heart longed for something to satisfy and assure him. Strange indeed were to be the incidents which should lead him to the answer.

CHAPTER NINE

A LIVING DEATH WITHIN MONASTERY WALLS

IF for Fray Luis there were disappointments in religion, there were compensating delights in his studies. Of the two courses open to him, a Doctorate in Philosophy or in Theology, he selected the former. His degree would come from the San Marcos University of Lima, founded by the Dominican Order in 1551, and the oldest institution of learning in the New World.

The routine hours of devotion meant little to him now. These were merely a pre-requisite to the delightful hours spent in Church history, logic, commentaries on the Gospels, apologetics, proofs of Christianity, and Dominican constitutions. The great tomes of Church lore and Catholic doctrine were each to receive him out of the crass world of religious superstition about him. In the *Summa Teologica*, the monumental and universe-embracing theology of that genius of the Church, Thomas Aquinas, he found the majesty as of a universe built by a master mind. Here was a vast domain of pure thought which the Church opened up to him. In these studies he found a zest of accomplishment which tended to hide from him at times the utter spiritual unreality which had so seriously threatened his new life.

So swiftly that he himself could scarcely believe it, the three years of the Simple Profession were ended, his studies successfully completed, and he was recommended for the Solemn Profession, in the taking of which vows the words "until death" should for ever close the door of the escape from his present life back into the world which, in the long ago, he had known. But the dignity of this Order is such that it is much to be desired. Its value far exceeds that of the seven other ordained Orders. Perhaps he would, in the opportunities for study, meditation, and research which would be his, penetrate the solemn mystery of life, come into the ineffable Presence, have communion and fellowship with God which, so far, had still been denied him.

On the day of the sacred investiture the Basilica (*Basilica del Santisimo Rosario*) was crowded with a concourse of worshippers, the incense rose in clouds from the altars, the music swelled from the organ, and the chants rose from the singing priests until the great stone edifice vibrated to the harmony. As one of the participants in the ceremony at this time was a Dominican bishop, El Obispo de Nuaras, this added unusual splendour to the event. Once more Fray Luis lay down before the altar in sign of utter death to all else; for the third time the burial service was read above him; and he rose a member of the Solemn Profession—only death could release him from these vows.

Now at last he had become a friar in his own right. Walter Manuel Montano was for ever dead—Fray Luis Beltran had taken his place. No longer did he live in separate rooms, eat by himself, worship in a chapel apart, but he became a fully accredited member of the Dominican community. For the first time he understood the real life of the priests. Whereas as a novitiate or member of the Simple Profession he had been under constant restraint and discipline, this was now entirely relaxed. Having now attained to this highest rank in the Order it was as though real saintliness were some doubtful good which might be dispensed with. Like the others, he found himself now free to break the rules as he pleased. Instead of a deeper holiness of life he found less; instead of increased sincerity, cynicism.

One day as Fray Luis was preparing the bread and wine for the priest who had been named to celebrate Mass, the other said to him, "And you, do you believe that this bread will actually become the body of Christ and this wine will become His blood?"

"Why, Father, of course!" exclaimed the astonished young monk of the Solemn Profession.

The other replied knowingly, shaking his head, as he replied, "Well, I do not."

"But then why do you celebrate Mass?" asked the younger man.

"Don't get excited," replied the older priest, "I have been much longer in the Order than you have. There are many things that we do not believe which we must teach the people. Transubstantiation is one of the cardinal doctrines of the

E

Church. If we were not to teach the common people this, then for them the Catholic Church would fall.''

Too overcome with surprise to answer, Fray Luis followed the older man into the chapel. As they went to the altar he was thinking of those blasphemous words, ''The bread was not His body; the wine was not His blood!'' Being a priest was, after all, only a way to make an easy living, and this sacred Mass an actor's trick to impress the ignorant rabble—a way to get their money when they felt the burden of their sins, or take estates from the rich when they feared for the soul of a loved one whose only future they thought would otherwise be purgatory.

As his companion elevated the host above the altar in the most solemn moment of saying Mass, Fray Luis looked at his face sharply. It seemed the countenance of a most holy saint glowing with loving reverence, and so devout was his attitude that one must have thought that he felt confident of holding in his hands, as in truth the Church professed he did, the Maker of heaven and earth and all that in them is—God, Creator, and Saviour of mankind.

When the ceremony had ended Fray Luis said to his companion, ''Father, you are nothing but a clown, that is all!''

Loud guffaws of laughter were the only answer.

Another day as Fray Luis was on his way to Confession he met one of the Order who had the reputation of not being a very moral priest. ''Where are you going?'' asked the latter.

''I am going to confess my sins, Father,'' returned Fray Luis.

''Foolish boy, do you still believe that the Confessor can forgive your sins?'' asked the friar.

''Why, yes, certainly, Father,'' replied the younger man in amazement.

''You are a fool,'' returned the other. ''When I used to hear Confession I would go to sleep in the confession box and pay no attention to the silly things.''

This was scarcely a spiritual preparation for the most solemn act of having one's sin dealt with in the only way which, according to the Church, a holy God could accept. But even this was nothing compared with the visit to the monastery in Lima of the Canonical Visitor, Father Domingo Fernandes, from Spain.

This man had been sent out by the generalissimo of the Dominican Order at Rome for the purpose of making a spiritual and moral survey of all the friars of the Order in Latin America. It was not only his privilege but his duty to call on priests one by one, place them under a most sacred vow of obedience, and order them to tell all that they knew about the moral life of their companions. It was inescapable. Failure meant excommunication, which only the Pope himself could remove. To speak falsehood here meant divine perjury which could damn the soul for ever.

Fray Luis was selected as secretary to this inquisitor. These duties gave him such a descent into a modern inferno as he in the darkest days of his bewildered disappointment had not imagined. It was his duty to copy down page after page of closely written matter relative to the secret lives of the priests, their follies and deceits, their betrayal of youthful innocence, their invasion of the sacred circle of the home, their debaucheries and licentiousness. Priests whom Fray Luis had looked upon as saints he now saw in the terrible light of reality. Some of the men whom he had most trusted as Confessors he feared as now he knew the depths of depravity to which they had sunk. A sadness unutterable settled upon his soul. And this was the fruit of all the sacrifice of home and friends and wealth, of all the study of theology, prayers, and holy Masses!

After the canonical visit and examination had been completed the Canonical Visitor called the priests into the choir loft and said, "I am sad because I find that the majority of you are deceivers. The white robe which you wear and which denotes purity of heart I find deeply stained by the black lives of evil which you lead. You must recover yourselves. Live lives of greater abstinence; employ fasting and penance. Be severe with yourselves lest the plagues of God fall upon you for all the evil you have committed, even as they did upon the priests of God in olden time when they profaned His sanctuary with unholy living and moral uncleanness."

Once before he had passed through something which had caused him the same kind of inward nausea that he felt now. Then, however, it could be thought of as a necessary means of preparing for the work of saving sinful men and women. That was when he was studying moral theology by San Alfonso

Maria de Ligorio. Here were described in vivid detail the most horrible crimes of boys and girls, of men and women. The task of the students was to determine the varying degrees of guilt, to distinguish the number of venial sins and number of mortal sins committed in any given case, so that later as Confessors when hearing similar things in real life they would know what questions to ask and what penance to assign.

When this study was begun the Professor noticed how fearful all were to speak of the unclean things. Most of the students said, "This is the most terrible study imaginable to me." Others said, "I feel that I have lost my dignity as a man to think of such things." The Professor would only laugh and say to them in Latin, the language in which the study was carried on, "Do not be ashamed. Bring more cases to class. Be more frank to speak of these things. You must know life if you are to help sinners."

The group of theological students were not angels. They had read things more licentious and degrading than the most pornographic novels. Not only that: they had to create imaginary cases and write them up in detail and tell the motives for the actions of the people concerned. It was opening a well of iniquity which flooded soul and mind. The reaction upon the priests was terrible. The revelations which came with the visit of the Canonical Visitor seemed to show that the priests were living all these very evils which they had then learned.

Fray Luis came to know also that it was common for the priests to quarrel with one another concerning who should hear the confession of the attractive young ladies who came to the Confessional. The monks admitted, with coarse jokes and meaning laughter, that what they enjoyed most was to question them about their moral character and their relationships with the young men. According to the law of the Order and of the Roman Catholic Church all statements in a Confessional are confidential (*Sigilo sacramental*) and must be kept secret, even at the price of death—better to lie than to reveal them. But in practice it was something entirely different, as the priests exchanged shameful confessions in the lives of their parishioners.

To Fray Luis the monastery appeared as a boat about to sink beneath the waves of sin. When the other priests learned of his preoccupations they would say to him, "Don't be a fool! Forget these things!" But how forget? His mind could do no other than dwell on them. Sin he saw triumphing in all those around him and filling his own heart and life—what else could the result be but the judgment of eternal death?

In the Bible he read, "He that believeth on the Son hath eternal life." But according to the ponderous theology which he had memorized it was impossible for one ever to know that one's sins were actually forgiven. "No one can ever know that he is saved," remarked one of the professors. "Not even the Pope knows whether he is saved until after he is dead." The only hope as a Dominican friar was that by praying to the Virgin of the Rosary until his last breath he might obtain her favour. He asked his Confessors, "How can one be sure of eternal life?" The answer always was, "There is no security for anyone."

The spiritual exercises of the monks were a means of moral discipline to create fear of sin and dread of the judgment. According to their teachings the wicked formed a great provision of firewood in hell. Gradually under the intense flame of torment they would become ashes, only to be reincarnated once more and burned again and again. There could be only the prospect either of purgatory or hell, and one was about as terrible as the other.

As a novitiate in his devotion to his studies he had known an experience of seeming peace and, kept from the revelation of what the true life of the priests was, he felt he was on his way to eternal life. Even when in the Simple Profession, he still had a feeling of assurance that he was to arrive at spiritual reality. But now as he entered full upon his career, his spiritual eye opened, his vision clear, and seeing in all its awfulness the moral degradation of the priests about him, he came into an epoch of spiritual torture. On the walls, the floor, the very sky he could see written in letters of fire one word—"Hell!"

There were several things he could have done. He might have become a practical atheist, hypocritically going through the performance of certain duties which were expected of him and teaching the people lies which he no longer believed. Others did this. He might have forgotten in indulgent licentiousness. Others did. But if he were to remain honest there was only one course open to him.

Santa Rosa of Lima, the beautiful saint of the nation of

Peru, had here, on these very grounds, shown the way. Days of fasting were hers and nights of vigil and prayers. It was here on this very site that she drove a stake into the ground and tied to it her long tresses so that, during the hours of the night, when overcome by slumber, as she fell forward the jerking upon her hair would arouse her to her spiritual duties. She had found God, had been canonized, was now receiving the homage of millions of hearts. He would take the way she had marked out. It would lead to peace and rest.

Night after night he removed the clothing and mattress from the bed and lay down upon the cold metal of the springs until it bit into his flesh and drove sleep from his eyes. If only he might have fellowship with God! Just once! If that smiling Virgin there on the wall would only speak to him—just once!

Also he began taking to the dinner-table tobacco ashes from his cigars to put into his food. If there were some particularly delicious soup he would pour salt into it until he would retch.

He went to a sacred grave,* a sepulchre in one of the cloisters in the chapel of the Solemn Profession. According to the history of the Church the dirt from the grave had miraculous qualities. He took the earth from over the body of this worthy, mixed it with tea or water, and drank it. He carried a quantity of it in his pocket, trusting thereby that he might at last be saved.

Driven constantly to greater efforts, he made a garment of rough material, formed of little wire hooks, and wore this about his waist and loins so that at every movement the flesh was galled or torn, causing a horror of pain and leaving his body a mass of wounds and sores.

Again emulating Santa Rosa, he went to one of the old buildings and made a heavy cross of rough beams, and there many nights in the darkness he would bear this cross until his shoulders would be bruised and his body racked with pain. But even with such suffering he found still that "these for sin could not atone".

He became so emaciated that his Superior remonstrated with him, "What is wrong? What are you doing? What makes you ill?" Finding him one day performing a particularly cruel penance he told him to stop it. "Give up such nonsense," he

* The grave of Beato Martin de Porres.

said; "that is meant only for the people outside who know no better." Some of the more serious monks, who, too, would have been glad to find what he was seeking, thought of Fray Luis as a spiritual guide because of these devotions, and sought his counsel. Others laughed at all this; but he could only wonder at their levity and their continued drunken revels in the face of these eternal problems which so oppressed his soul. One old monk remonstrated, "Stop all this! Others who have done this have married or become military men."

The Virgin smiled as coyly, or was it, as indifferently, as ever. Either she did not see or did not care.

CHAPTER TEN

"LITTLE HELL" POINTS THE WAY TO HEAVEN

IF there was one consuming passion in Fray Luis' life greater than religion it was literature. Accustomed at an early age to seeing his father absorbed in some volume of ancient philosophy or modern science, and from his earliest days used to reading for himself the best that a great library of a wealthy home could accord; it was but natural that at an early age he should have dedicated much of this thought and energy to the art of writing.

By the time he had reached the age of twenty-three years he was an accomplished journalist in his own right and earning a considerable amount through his pen. Under the heading "The International Moment" he became a columnist for South American periodicals. Here he treated historical, patriotic, religious, and political subjects of world significance with such tremendous vitality and passionate earnestness that now years afterwards the files of clippings make absorbing reading.

As priors do not always enjoy having their own dignity and authority overshadowed by a mere friar whose name comes too easily and frequently to men's lips it became necessary for Fray Luis to adopt two pseudonyms under which his material was sold—El Duque de Siultno Magno, and Ruiz de Oropeza.

Hating Chile as fervently as when a lad he had held forth before his Uncle Eliodoro Villazon, former President of the Republic, he could now furbish his sword on the front page of the dailies and pour forth the vials of his wrath in apocalyptic denunciations. From a religious standpoint his poems were as important perhaps as any part of his work, though the spurious traditions of the Church were also enriched by his imagination.

The Pope had decided to canonize Beato Martin de Porres, who had been a lay member of the Dominican Order in Lima four hundred years before. However, it was necessary for him to have the history of the individual who was to be canonized as authority for such an act, and as proof of his saintliness and the miracles which God through him had been pleased to perform.

As a matter of fact, no one really knew much of anything about Beato Martin de Porres, which perhaps made it all the easier to canonize him, for certainly not one could prove that he did not deserve this honour. After all available materials had been placed in Fray Luis' hands for the task of producing the biography he saw that the larger part of such a book must be purely invention. But as the end justifies the means in the Catholic faith, the canonization of a worthy man would justify a lie. As a holy end was in view Fray Luis could quiet his conscience, and not only that but he was ordered to do so by Fray Domingo Lliarta, who was in charge of the campaign for the sanctification or beatification of Martin de Porres. Also everything must finally be approved by the theologians of the monastery upon whose judgment he relied.

In the series of miracles Fray Luis invented was one showing the humility of Beato Martin de Porres when working as a barber in the monastery. According to the story, one of the friars, a very vain fellow, wanted to have his hair in curls, and more than just the three fingers' width around the shaven crown, as provided in the constitution. He was so enraged when he saw the way in which his hair had been cut that he started to insult Beato Martin, calling him "Negro", for he was a mulatto. But Martin with an indulgent smile wrapped a towel about his head, and when he removed it the man's head was covered with heavy curls, much to his pleasure.

There were also pictured the sick who were relieved when they cried out in their pain, "Fray Beato, help me!" At once his spirit appeared and gave them water, food, or medicine as needed. This miracle took place in China, India, and Africa as well as in South America, for his spirit appeared quite impartially wherever needy people called for him.

One day Beato Martin, as the narrative unfolded, was feeding his dog when a cat came up and looked on longingly. He called to the cat, "Come, Brother Cat, and eat!" The dog permitted the cat to eat the food with him. Spying a rat in the corner, Martin called to this little creature also, "Come, Brother Rat, and eat!" for he called all animals "Brother", and there were dog, cat, and rat, all eating out of a common dish at the feet of this good and holy man!

The history of Beato Martin de Porres, as thus fabricated by Fray Luis, was unanimously approved by the holy fathers of the Dominican Order; was published as written; and circulated through South America: and on the basis of this volume the Roman Pope began the work of canonizing this humble servant of the early Dominican friars of Lima, Peru.

Always a devotee of the library and by nature studious, he was named to take charge of this place, the largest institution of its kind in South America. So it was with the delight of a connoisseur and the joy of being the youngest ever named to this responsible post that he assumed the position of head librarian. Not only was he responsible for the volumes on hand, but he had oversight also of the expenditure of thousands of dollars each year in acquiring new and better books.

The Dominican library was housed in a long, tall, modernly-equipped hall. Ordinarily only priests were admitted to this room, though students from the University were also granted permission for special study and research.

From many standpoints this appointment seemed a favourable omen. It came shortly after he had entered upon the Solemn Profession, when the revelations of moral and spiritual failure in the life of the monastery were pressing him hardest. It became a means which he greatly welcomed of making his connection with the Catholic Church more tolerable. It also gave him untrammelled opportunity to revel in the books of his choice. He particularly enjoyed the older volumes written in Latin and the intimate papers of the Church Fathers.

Of all the writers he felt greatest interest in Saint Thomas Aquinas, who was perhaps the outstanding intellect of the Catholic Church. Always before beginning his studies it was Fray Luis' custom to pray to Aquinas, and his triumphs in writing he attributed to the direct assistance which he thus received. Perhaps there was prophecy in this, for many students affirm that had Protestantism been even humanly conceivable in the time of Thomas Aquinas he would probably have been one of the early reformers.

In his new office Fray Luis became responsible for "Little Hell", which consisted of a room at the end of the main library entered by only one door. It was filled with non-Catholic or condemned, religious books, particularly those of the Protestant sects, which could only be consulted by special permission under the direction of the Superior of the Order. Not even Fray Luis, the head librarian, had any right so much as to open one of these volumes.

One day while Fray Luis was overseeing the task of dusting "Little Hell", as he passed down the stacks he noticed standing out from the line of books one which had not been properly put back into place. He paused and, as he reached out to adjust it, his eye caught the title, *Nights with the Romanists*. The titled burned itself into Fray Luis' mind. It suggested the rather novel possibility that the hated and feared Protestants might have something to say to Roman Catholics in defence of their position. He shoved the book into place and went on.

As the lay worker continued the dusting in another part of the room Fray Luis could not forget the book which had so curiously secured his attention. He thought he might return and, unobserved, look at the prologue at least. He did so. The preface but whetted his desire to read more. He was alone. Quickly he thrust the book under his monk's habit, where the girdle tied about his waist kept it from falling to the floor. He called abruptly to his assistant, "Let us close up for this afternoon. You may begin work here in the morning."

In his room it was necessary to find a place where the prying eyes of the Superior would not discover the volume. It was placed under the jar for carrying out waste water. To read it was of course another matter. To do so he must risk the possibility of detection. Smoking a large cigar and his heart jumping at every noise, he began reading the first chapter dealing with salvation by faith.

As a matter of fact, the book did not bring him peace. It brought him only greater confusion. He felt a little like the judge who said that he preferred to hear only one side of a case, as it was much easier in that way to render a decision. If before he had been in the dark, that darkness was now deepened. He was for ever having quickly to hide the volume. When he reached the chapter on the Virgin Mary where the Protestant writer frankly admitted that while the evangelicals venerated, they could not worship her, Fray Luis wanted to throw the volume out of the window. When he had finished *Nights with the Romanists* it was stealthily returned to its accustomed place in "Little Hell".

Another volume which fell into his hands at this time and which greatly interested him was written by a Catholic father, Father Francisco de Paula Vigil, concerning the rights of priests and inveighing against the Roman Church. The Pope had immediately excommunicated him. But the doughty author wrote, "You may excommunicate me, but God does not excommunicate me." Such daring amazed Fray Luis. As an extra precaution with this volume he had written the name of his father around the edge of the pages. One day, even though it was in its accustomed place of hiding in his cell, the sharp eyes of the prior discovered it. "It is my father's book," said Fray Luis. "See, his name is upon it. I keep it hidden because it is a forbidden book and I did not wish the other friars to see it." However, the Prior took it to destroy.

This book had seemed strangely related to what Fray Luis found in *Nights with the Romanists*. He sought out this forbidden volume once more and took it to his room. He particularly wished to read and study the chapter dealing with Mary.

One day during the quiet hour, when profound silence reigned throughout the monastery, as he was reading he fell asleep.

When he awoke the door was open and the Superior standing in the doorway. "Why do you not sleep in your bed, Fray Luis, and not at your desk?" he asked kindly.

"Why, I am reading a book." Fray Luis scarce knew what to answer. "A book, you see, I am reading a book——" His confusion and nervousness betrayed him.

The Prior came over and picked up the tell-tale volume. "Fray Luis, you are reading a condemned book of the Protestants." He shook his head sadly. "We trusted you by making you librarian. If you were any other than whom you are by birth and appointment your punishment would be much more severe. But you shall lie at the door tonight and permit the friars to walk into the dining-hall over your prostrate body. During the meal you shall kiss the feet of all. And then again you shall lie in the doorway and all shall pass out over your body. You will continue this for one week, Fray Luis!"

For a week, at each mealtime, the solemn, white-robed group

walked into the dining-hall over his prostrate body; alone on bended knees he would eat his meal off a little table in front of the pulpit from which the Bible was read during the meal hour; and then he would lie down once more and permit them to pass out over him. Some of the monks, as he went round under the unoccupied side of the narrow table which faced the centre of the room, would motion to him to kiss their scapulary instead of their feet; and some, as they passed out, would not place their full weight upon him. However, his first adventure in the doctrine of salvation by faith was not yielding the peaceable fruits of righteousness. A ferment, a storm, had been unleashed in his mind.

One day in the halls he met a lay member of the Order coming in from the market-place with his purchases. In his hand he held a little book. "What is that?" commanded Fray Luis.

The man handed it over. "It's just a little religious book that they gave me down there."

Fray Luis read its title, *The Salvation Army Song Book*. "Fool!" he said, "don't you know that this is a condemned book?"

The man was frightened at such a suggestion. "What can I do?" he inquired. "I did not mean to bring a condemned book here?"

"That is all right," replied Fray Luis consolingly. "Just leave that to me and I will take care of it for you." He walked off with the treasure trove thus easily separated from its owner.

In his room he read the book of simple gospel songs. He felt his soul truly stirred by their message.

He lent the volume to one of the novitiates, Fray Alberto Llamas, who afterwards escaped from the monastery. The man went to South Peru, was converted to the gospel, and became an evangelical Christian. Such was the influence of those hardy Salvation Army missionary groups, some of whose early leaders sealed their ministry with their own life's blood, reaching even to those within the walls of the convent.

So great was the mental darkness, so intense the agony, that Fray Luis at times reached a desperate willingness to try anything religious if it promised spiritual reality.

When the Dominicans planned to repair the old cloister of the monastery they employed an outstanding architect, Señor

Revoredo. As Fray Luis had defended in published articles certain artistic contentions of this man it was but natural that they should wish to meet each other.

In their conversation Fray Luis revealed his troubled heart. "You should be a spiritualist," said the architect positively. "It is the only way. It is through spiritualism that I find satisfaction."

"Do you have peace?" asked Fray Luis wistfully.

"Yes. I am entirely satisfied."

"Do you think I could find peace and satisfaction this way?"

"Certainly! Many others do. It is very simple. Get a table made without iron nails. Take it to your room. Put paper upon it and take a pencil in your hand. Then invoke the spirits of the dead. They will come and write messages to you from the spirit world."

That night Fray Luis sat in his monk's cell with a wooden table made without nails in front of him. He invited communication from the spirit of Napoleon, Bolivar, or San Martin. Finally he consented to accept the services of any spirit that might be willing to oblige him. But nothing happened, neither spirit, sprite, nor fairy came to bring him the longed-for message from the other world.

The next day he chided his friend, the architect. "But you have not done it right. I forgot to tell you that you must not do this on holy ground. Go to some place that has not been consecrated. Remove your holy garb. Then you will receive the message that you need. The spirits will come and move your fingers, writing for you."

That evening as soon as possible Fray Luis stole away from the convent out to the chicken-house, where he set up the table made without iron nails, took paper and pencil, and waited expectantly. Finally, despairing that the spirit of any human being would respond to his entreaty, he prayed that the devil might come. Nothing happened.

Now, however, the sinfulness of his act dawned upon him. According to the constitution of the Dominican Order he was automatically excommunicated from the Church and from God. Fear seized his heart. Hell seemed pressing upon him. He must make confession. He sought out one of the most respected monks. His Confessor ordered him at once to cease from all spiritual exercises and to remain in his cell. "No one but the Pope himself can forgive you," he explained.

The matter was presented to the Archbishop and then referred to the Representative of the People in Peru. After considerable delay a favourable answer came from the Vatican. Fray Luis was called to the Confessional, and after confession heard these words, "By the authority of the Pope, our most holy father, I absolve you from your sins."

So he found that even the devil would have nothing to do with him!

CHAPTER ELEVEN

IN THE TEMPLE OF THE SUN

LIKE many another man Fray Luis thought that he could run away from trouble. He asked for, and was granted, a tranfer to Cuzco, ancient capital of the Incas. Here the monastery had been built upon the foundations of the Temple of the Sun. This was the scene of bygone glory when the Incas worshipped in their "Ingot of Gold", a building whose walls, columns, furniture even, were all of shining gold, and above whose altar hung an immense golden image of the sun just where the first rays of the dawn might fall upon it. Here the Incas, after worshipping in the temple of gold, had gone down steps and walks of gold to bathe in cisterns of gold in water brought through golden pipes, and had then walked in gardens where flowers, vines, wheat, sheep, and shepherds were of purest beaten gold. And why not? The Incas were the "children of the sun". Gold was the "tears of the sun" and therefore belonged to them. The native people, having no use for the yellow metal, gladly gave it to those who brought to them the arts of civilization.

But how swiftly that gold disappeared! He recalled the insatiable thirst of the Spaniard—that terrible, consuming fever which only gold could cure. How quickly this scene of unexampled splendour had been destroyed, the walls stripped, the altars desecrated—ruin, destruction, bloodshed, lust!

Strange, thought Fray Luis, as he walked through these scenes of former glory, that a priest, the first Bishop of Cuzco, Superior of the Dominican Order in that land, the infamous Valverde, should have been the leader in this pillage and sacrilege. He had zealously given Christian baptism to the defeated Inca Atahualpa, and then, as a matter of strategy, permitted him to be strangled to death. He had looked on nonchalantly as the Spaniards quarrelled over the beautiful Virgins of the Sun who came forth from their convent by the sacred lake to bewail the fallen Emperor and protest the "Christian" rites by which he was being buried. But the ways of the Church must not be questioned—the will of its leaders was the will of God!

Here in Cuzco he was returning one day from a trip to the country where he had taken a group of students for their period of recreation when he passed a small doorway above which was a sign reading, "Evangelical Mission". He crossed himself devoutly to keep away any malevolent influence. He knew that these people were worshippers of the devil in person. He had preached this to large congregations. All good Catholics knew it to be so. This was the first time that he had, knowingly, come so close to any of these heretics.

Among those who began coming to young Fray Luis for spiritual help was a Señorita Casanova, daughter of a very much respected family, who for many years had been a school teacher. Previously she had been a very close friend of the Superior, and there were those who criticized their relationship. She was also on rather intimate terms with another of the fathers, Father Morales, and brought gifts to both of these men indiscriminately, causing considerable jealousy between them.

One day as Fray Luis was returning to the monastery with Father Castro, after having sung Mass in the convent of the nuns, an attractive woman stood in the outside doorway. As they approached her Father Castro greeted her warmly and said, "Señorita Casanova, I want you to meet one of the best poets in our monastery, or for that matter in our Order, Fray Luis."

"Yes, I have wanted to meet you," she answered, taking his hand in both of hers; "I have read your writings with interest."

As a result of this meeting the Señorita Casanova began to include Fray Luis among those receiving the gifts which she brought to the monastery. The result was bitter resentment from the Superior and from Father Morales. Because of the difference in their years Fray Luis always addressed this *señorita* as a mother and she treated him as a son. The embittered friars, however, wrote a letter to which Fray Luis' name was forged, hoping thus to create trouble between them. The young man's answer to them was, "My friendship with this woman is different from that you wish with her. I am as a son to her and respect her as a mother, but your wishes are immoral." Their deepened enmity could be the only result.

Here in Cuzco Fray Luis' religion was put to another test

F

and seemed to fail. On several occasions in Lima he had seen priests die. The mask of any seeming strength or consolation which religion might have afforded them was torn away. Death for them was a hideous, grudging surrender to the king of terrors. But when Father Castro, of Cuzco, became ill Fray Luis felt that religion should now be vindicated as victory over the last enemy. In the first place he regarded Father Castro as the most holy, saintly man he had ever met. His life had been given to praying, fasting, sacred reading, penance, and confession. Innumerable Masses had been offered for him. Surely now there would be some indication of the divine favour.

But such was not the case. For this man, shut away from friends and family, without the loving hand of wife or daughter to soothe him, or a manly son at his side to serve him, was dying amid the white-and-black-robed members of the Order, with the utter desperation of a condemned man who had no hope. His face was already like that of one damned. His room was terrible with nameless fear. It was something to be forgotten as quickly as possible. His religion did nothing for him when he needed it most. The Church, of course, promised to assist him after he entered purgatory, but how to do anything now, how to resolve the uncertainty and doubt and bring to his troubled soul assurance was entirely beyond its power.

As a result of the death of his friend, Fray Luis began smoking as never before. When he awakened in the morning a cigar was his first thought. He lighted a fresh one through the day with the dying embers of the one before until time for retirement at night. This brought a narcotic relief and helped him to forget.

Fray Luis, who came to the monastery seeking peace and salvation, found only the bitter truth of that saying, "The friars enter without knowing each other, live without loving one another, and die without weeping for each other."

He still wrote the fulsome articles for the Press, defending and extolling the Church, but his poems of this period betray the deepest sorrow and spiritual anguish. Light had turned to darkness indeed in this Temple of the Sun. The monastery became a prison. In one of his most beautiful poems he wrote of the song-bird that hung in a cage in front of his window and whose life seemed a type of his own—only the bird had a song and he had none.

CHAPTER TWELVE

THE MONK WHO LIVED AGAIN

WHEN the Holy Spirit sought a leader for the early Church He reached through the walls of wealth, tradition, ecclesiastical preferment, and political prestige and made a Saul of Tarsus into Paul the Apostle.

Walter Manuel Montano was also bound by the walls of social caste and traditional religion, from which, it seemed, there could never be escape. There was no way by which he might be evangelized. No missionary could ever penetrate the circles where he moved, no gospel preacher there make his message known. And yet these impenetrable walls could offer no resistance to the Spirit of God, which through the years troubled him and drove him towards a spiritual discovery which should satisfy his deepest needs.

On January 1st, 1927, Fray Luis' birthday was being celebrated by the Dominican monks of the Monastery of Cuzco. But the one who was being thus honoured felt none of the joy which seemed to animate his companions, who, forgetting their sacerdotal decorum, drank, sang love songs, danced with one another, and generally gave way to the pranks which wine and good fellowship might suggest. In the midst of the hilarity he sat in a corner of the large hall where the monks met in their hours of diversion, with an aching sadness that he could not hide. With half-drunken laughter and mocking jest the others sought to secure his participation. But what was there in all this for a soul in spiritual agony, athirst for companionship with the living God?

So thoroughly delighted were the monks with the party that they decided to continue the festivities on the following evening. Though the rules of the Order were for all noise and conversation to cease at nine-thirty o'clock, this was forgotten as the unrestrained jollity of worldly songs and drunken jesting took the place of the supposed solemnity of the priest. The Superior of the Chapter, who, on one occasion, under the influence of liquor, had attacked him, came up to Fray Luis and tried to get him to forget his melancholy and join in the sport. "Come, drink," he said, "and forget your troubles!" Fray

Luis felt more like weeping than sharing in this artificial hilarity.

A thousand confused thoughts seemed surging through his mind, but watching the foolishness and listening to the maudlin sentiment of his companions as the rich liquor increasingly deprived them of their reason, it was as though a refrain of which he had been largely unconscious, but which had always been beating upon his heart, became suddenly audible to his consciousness. Over and over again the impulse surged through his mind, "You must escape from all this! Get out! Go! Run away! There's nothing here for you!" But where? What of the danger? And what of the future?

A book out of "Little Hell" had spoken to Fray Luis. A sign along the way had one day excited his curiosity. The Protestants, as he well knew and had many times preached, worshipped the devil in person. But what of it? Perhaps they had peace—he had none. Perhaps there was a joyous abandonment in giving oneself to the devil, though sold to him for eternity. Nothing could be worse than the living hell of the monastery life, the fearful torture of conscience, the fruitless round of penance, the fitful attempts to forget. Suddenly the resolution formed itself in his mind. It was as though he had always planned it but only now became conscious of his purpose. He would go to the Protestants. He would ask them for an answer to life. If they could give it, all was well; he, too, would worship the devil in person. If they could not, nothing was lost—he would fight his way through, and God or the devil would somehow keep him out of the hands of the Dominican monks.

It was almost with complacency now that he watched the antics of his religious comrades; the coarse, at times vile, jokes ceased to wound him; the gusts of loud laughter swept over him and left him unmoved. As soon as he could do so inconspicuously he slipped away from the party which was being held in his honour.

Once in his cell there were many decisions to be made quickly. What things should he take? Of course the library of books built up through the years with his father's money must be sacrificed. His manuscripts of poems and articles were his first thought, then clothes and personal articles which would be needed on the outside. To his knowledge he had never seen a Protestant, let alone associated with one. What were they like? What, after all, might he not be getting into? But a voice seemed to be talking to him assuringly, tenderly, "Go there! They will receive you! That is your place!" He looked up at the Virgin on the wall, his one love and faithful companion during the years. She only smiled as always. Why had she never spoken to him? Well, it was speak now or never.

He turned out the light as he heard the friars coming from their late roistering. A street light above a high and unscaleable wall which surrounded the court just outside the window shone through into his room. That near was he to liberty. He looked out into the shadowy orchard. It reminded him of his father's home in Cochabamba, where in the garden was a tree, for him the tree of the knowledge of good and evil, from which so many times he had dropped to liberty. But no such simple escape was possible here.

The other wall of the *patio* separated the convent of the nuns from the monastery of the monks. There is a Spanish saying, "Between the nun and the monk let there be a wall of cement and rock." How little good rock walls did in assuring the keeping of their vows by certain priests, he remembered rather bitterly as he studied the situation. He was forced to the conclusion that only one way of escape remained—the rather dangerous expedient of following the man who awakened the monks in the morning and taking the chance of finding the lad with the keys whom he felt certain he could make obey him. Of one thing he was certain; escape, for him, was inevitable.

His plan of action had been thoroughly thought out. The next morning he carried it swiftly into action and with what success we already know. When he had passed through the last of the closed doors which stood between him and freedom the cold breeze from off the Andes quickened him into action. As he bade Pedro, the awakener, goodbye in the gathering light of the dawn he started off rapidly down Santo Domingo Street.

When he reached the street door of the mission property it was shut. He pounded upon it. A strange sight indeed was this, a monk in the full regalia of his Order standing at the Protestant's door and calling for admittance. A gardener, early at his task inside, replied, "But, Father, this is not the Catholic monastery. This is a Protestant mission." Doubtless, thought he, here is a poor priest, drunk after an all-night escapade, and in his delirium he has mistaken our mission for his church.

Fray Luis pounded more heartily than before. "Yes, yes, I know it is the Protestant mission. That is why I am here. Where is the chief of your Order?" He did not know in what terms to ask for the minister in charge.

"Oh, it is too early for our chief," answered the gardener.

Just then a young man of thirty-five years of age put his head out of the window of the mission home and; evidently having overheard the conversation, shouted, "Wait a moment and I will come down." By so narrow a margin, perhaps, did Fray Luis come to missing the Wicket Gate which leads to the Celestial City.

A few minutes later the Rev. Charles A. Patton of the Evangelical Union of South America appeared on the steps of the mission house and came down the walk towards the gate to admit the Dominican monk who was standing there. This missionary was a tall, well-built man, the kind who would be appreciated on any college athletic field. He was smiling kindly, and there was about him that strange radiance and buoyancy which was already telling upon him. Though he had scarcely reached the zenith of manhood's powers his nervous system was already shattered by the labours he had borne. Within four years' time, after a futile effort to regain his health, he was destined to lay down his life as a good soldier of Jesus Christ in the depths of the Brazilian wilderness. But here he was this early dawn, upon the great adventure of his life—landing in the gospel net a man who, years after he himself had faded from the memory of any except intimates, would be shaking Latin America with his God-given messages. He was a bearer of the light, one of that army to which Robert Louis Stevenson refers as "Lantern-bearers". He left behind him no monument but living stones in the ever-growing temple of the risen Christ.

In the living-room of the mission home at Cuzco the two men stood facing each other. Both represented the flower of their own race and culture. The dark-haired, brown-eyed monk of Castillian blood gazed searchingly, questioningly, with a fierce demand for spiritual reality into the blue eyes of the Saxon missionary, which now glowed with a strange, tender light.

Fray Luis was not given to indecision. "For years," he said, addressing the stranger before him who, however, in that very moment somehow ceased to seem other than a friend, "I have desired to find peace and salvation. In seeking these I went to the Monastery of Santo Domingo. Seven years I remained there. But instead of the peace which I so anxiously sought I have been disappointed and deceived. Now I come to you, that you may please tell me, by all that you hold dear in this world, whether you have peace in your heart. If you have, tell me. If not, for God's sake tell me that. I beg of you do not deceive me again!"

Tears were rolling down the cheeks of Charles A. Patton as he reached out his arms and placed them on the shoulders of the earnest priest before him and, gazing sympathetically into the other's searching eyes, replied, "I cannot discuss theology nor doctrine with you, but I can tell you that years ago I came to Christ Jesus with my heart burdened with sin and filled with unrest. I confessed all my sins to Jesus, my Lord, and He forgave them every one, and now I have peace and salvation. He will do the same for you."

It was five-thirty o'clock on the morning of January 3rd, 1927, when these two men knelt down before the living Saviour. There was no argument. There were no long explanations. Protestant and Catholic apologetics had no place here. They were praying—the one out of long years of fellowship with his Friend, his Guide, his Saviour—the other beginning, stumbling, falteringly, to pray—really to pray—for the first time in his life. It would have been natural for him to fall into the long, beautifully-worded prayers which he had so laboriously memorized and upon which he had spent hours daily in meaningless repetition. But such praying would not do now. He was through with it, sick of it. He, Walter Manuel Montano, had for years been buried under the habit of a Dominican friar, hidden behind the name of Fray Luis, separated from the world by artificial walls which had thrust him back upon the tempest of his own unquieted soul and but mocked him with the futile emptiness of a sacrifice which, instead of enriching life, increased its needs. But now deep spoke to deep as his spirit struggled free into the liberty of personal intercourse with his God and Saviour.

From the broken depths of Fray Luis' being were bursting

forth confessions of one who, for the first time, sees himself in the clear light of God's holiness. The divine Iconoclast was breaking down and casting out the cherished idols of his heart, the Spirit of the living God was melting him, the fire of conviction was burning through his self-righteousness, sin was being brought to the light of his understanding that the blood of Christ might by actual faith be appropriated and his guilt covered once and for all. Tears were streaming from those eyes which had for so long been straining to catch a smile from the Virgin's face. He was talking to Someone now! The ineffable Presence was an unquestioned reality. A Voice was speaking to him. His heart was lighter, the burden was lifting, an unutterable peace and quiet were settling down through his inmost being, a spring of joy seemed to have broken loose deep within his heart, and the living waters of which the Master spoke had already begun to spring up unto eternal life.

The two men had lost all count of time. For a while they had lived in eternity. But prayer was now ended. The answer had come. Fray Luis had indeed died, not upon the altars of an apostate Church but upon Calvary with his Christ. But he, too, had risen to newness of resurrection life, not through the mumbled ritual of a sinful priest, but through the power of the matchless life of One who had died but lived again, and to whose life-giving touch he thrilled as did those who knew Him in Galilee long centuries past.

The two men rose to their feet. The floor was wet with their tears. It was ten-thirty o'clock. They had been on their knees five hours. The miracle had happened. Jesus had found another life in which to live incarnate. Seven long years in hell had ended. A new man could witness to Christ's victory. Instead of the devil he was worshipping Christ, a living Christ who moved his heart to unspeakable joy.

It was breakfast time now. Together they walked to the table—the missionary and the white-robed priestly figure. There was now no time for practical details.

Walter Manuel Montano began to pull from the capacious folds of his Dominican robes various things which he had hurriedly stuffed in there that morning. When Mr. Patton saw a pair of nearly new football shoes dragged out, he asked good-naturedly, "Say, what are those?"

"Well," confessed the former Fray Luis, a little hesitantly,

"I didn't know what life would be like on the outside. So I just brought them along thinking I might need to sell them to get something to eat.

"How could I ever have believed what I did about you?" continued the new convert. "I used to think that you worshipped the devil in person. I thought you had a crucifix in the window pointing towards a river or perhaps a canal, and that there you confessed your sins and would blow them out of the window hoping that the water would take them away. In fact, I brought a crucifix with me so that, in case I needed it in your worship, I would have it."

Mr. Patton smiled. There was no need to answer. The answer had come. Instead of being worshipped, the "Prince of this World" had been judged and cast out. Jesus, the Prince of Peace, had set up His kingdom in Fray Luis' heart—Dr. Walter Manuel Montano, Protestant leader and preacher of the everlasting gospel, had been born, though he could not then, and it was best that he could not, know the fierce fires of persecution through which he would be called upon to pass.

CHAPTER THIRTEEN

THE FIRES OF A MODERN INQUISITION

"WHAT a fool I have been!" Walter Manuel Montano, the former Fray Luis, many times would say. "I should have been a physician, a lawyer, a professional man, but I am nothing but a priest, and now I do not wish to be that."

Mr. Patton would laugh in his friendly way. "No! Don't talk like that," he would counsel. "God has given you your providential preparation for your destined life work. Thank Him for it!"

But one thing was certain—he had peace, real peace. There was no doubt about it—he was an absolutely new man. The fear of hell was gone. Heaven seemed already begun in his heart. He was positively happy.

As for ordinary street clothes, there was nothing for it at first but to wear some of Mr. Patton's. But the missionary's height was such that some ludicrous combinations resulted from Walter Manuel's attempt to wear them. A blue coat was found, however, which did fairly well, though the sleeves were too long and the waist and tails failed to find their proper elevation.

His monkish crown was covered with a three or four days' growth of hair surrounded by shaggy locks. "Shall I call a barber?" Mrs. Patton inquired. "No, you do it," Walter Manuel replied, laughing. And so the longer hair was pruned back with a pair of shears to the approximate length of that on the crown and left to grow out with it.

He still enjoyed carrying his baston, the sign of the doctorate degree in philosophy from the San Marcos University, which was given him by the Regent of Studies of the Dominican Order of Peru. He also used high collars with turned-back corners, and wore spats. While in the monastery he would many times go without shaving for days and without caring for his appearance, a part of personal negation, in his search for holiness. Still he had clothes of many different kinds, fitting his station in life, and only gradually could he leave many of his former habits of dress, which came both from the social life to which he was accustomed as a boy and as a member of the wealthy Dominican Order of monks.

One morning Mr. Patton remarked gladly, "I see that you are not smoking now."

"No, that has left me completely. I do not care to smoke any more." Though no one had urged such a conviction upon him, gradually, as new interests filled the horizon of his life, his addiction to the use of tobacco, which had in his former life offered a partial form of escape from reality, dropped away from him.

"Thank God for this," replied Mr. Patton. "We have been praying about this." Yes, life had changed for Fray Luis. Old things had passed, were passing, away. All things were becoming new; he, himself, was indeed a new creature in Christ Jesus.

At times in these first days of his new-found joy Dr. Walter Manuel Montano would ponder: "I wanted to be a religious man. I wanted to find God. Why did God permit me to enter the monastery? Why did not His Holy Spirit lead me in my early, impressionable years directly into a Protestant Church?" But gradually he came to see that this was also of God's planning so that he might know the Roman Catholic religion, know the hearts and souls and minds of the people among whom he was to work as a minister of the gospel, and thereby know how to touch the deepest chords of their hearts. The severe intellectual training and his experience in literature and journalism were all very real values also which had accrued from those rigorous years.

Walter Manuel discovered that things began to happen immediately in the monastery as soon as his escape became known. A lay member of the Order reported his absence to the Superior. The only one who had the keys on the night of his escape was the lad who had assisted him. He was put in irons and tortured with the inquisitorial instruments of the Dominicans. They put him finally into a special cell, where he was beaten with poles. They squeezed his hands until they were bleeding and he was frenzied with pain. "Turn me loose," he shouted, "and I will tell you where he is. He left a valise with me; you may take it. I saw him go down the streets of Santo Domingo towards *Monjaspata*."

A lady reported to the monks that Fray Luis had turned

into the gate of the Evangelical Mission. Spies were sent to watch whether or not he was actually living with the hated Protestants.

His valise, which he had supposed contained extra clothing, in reality had been filled with his precious manuscripts, and this fruit of years of labour was confiscated by the prior. This loss caused him more mental distress than any other.

The lad who had opened the doors for the early morning escape was dismissed in disgrace from the monastery.

The Dominican priests felt at first that it would after all be a comparatively easy task to convince him of the error of his ways and re-convert him to the life of the monastery. They had everything to offer him—it was certain no one but a fool would stay among the impecunious Protestants.

The Brothers of the Franciscan Order also sent a delegation to talk with him. They invited him to dine with them, and, as Walter Manuel had intimate friends among them, he consented. "If you do not go back with the Dominicans, come with us," they urged.

He told them of the deep happiness he had found in his new religious experience.

"Are you sure? Are you really sure?" they asked with pathetic eagerness.

"If I were not sure," he answered, "I would not be there among the Protestants."

While waiting for the dinner hour in the quiet of the Franciscans' library he asked for pen and paper and wrote "Light and Shadow", an article published throughout the Press of Latin America.

After dinner the priests gathered about him asking many questions. How do the Protestants live? What do they eat? How do they dress? What kind of meeting do they have? How do they preach?

They were so deeply interested that a number wrote to him later, asking if he had a place for them among the Protestants. Their hearts also craved the peace which had come to him. But he always replied to them that unless they had a real heart conviction to leave their former life and in spite of any possible hardship to become Protestants they had better remain where they were. He knew all too well that only as a deep, powerful experience of the regenerating power of the Holy

Spirit could change their lives would they be able to bear the
tests and remain true to their new faith. Even Christ in the
days of His earthly ministry sent some disciples away because
their conversion was not deep enough to stand reality.

Not a few of the priests who had been close friends of Fray
Luis were so deeply stirred by his action that they requested
that a way be found for them secretly to hear the preaching
of the Word, and so· a curtain was hung in the mission hall
in such a way that they could, unobserved, slip in and out by
a side entrance.

People everywhere talked of the strange happenings in their
religious world and pointed out the Dominican priest who had
become a Protestant.

Certain rumours, however, were beginning to be rather
persistently circulated. A Franciscan friar had gone at night
to the Convent of Santa Clara. One of the nuns managed to
climb over the wall and to escape with her religious paramour.
But though the truth was known to all who cared to seek the
facts, still the suggestion made by the priests had grown into
a report that Dr. Montano had taken this woman and was
keeping her in the house of the Protestants.

He was also accused of another incident which occurred at
this time. The secretary of the Bishop of Arequipa ran away
with a married woman whose confessions he had heard
regularly for years. The rumour spread that Fray Luis was the
guilty individual. The political authorities themselves replied
to this accusation by arresting the guilty pair and bringing
them back as prisoners.

Almost immediately he began assisting the one who had
guided him into this new spiritual life by accompanying Mr.
Patton everywhere distributing literature, giving out tracts,
acting as colporteur, preaching, and visiting in the homes.

"You shall remain in charge of the work when I leave,"
Mr. Patton declared. Walter Manuel would only say, "No,
not that, I do not know enough. I am too young."

"Then you shall be my co-pastor."

"I am not worthy," was the answer. But despite his pro-
testations he was named to act as assistant.

He went to Urubamba to preach. The mission was too small
for the crowds which came. It was necessary to rent a larger
hall. The first night there were among the crowd army officers,

local authorities, and political leaders. Even the parish priest, who was also the town's mayor, was among those present. This latter called out during the sermon, "Did you learn to preach like this in the monastery?" As this priestly official continued to badger Dr. Montano he finally challenged him to a public debate in the field of either theology or philosophy. But the priest immediately found a perfectly good excuse for not accepting, as "the bishop had not given him permission to discuss religion publicly".

Dr. Montano was asked to pay for a licence to preach, which was entirely contrary to the law. He was accused before the Prefect and Governor of the State of Cuzco for fomenting a seditious meeting, encouraging communism, and destroying public order.

The secretary of the Prefect, who was a fanatical Roman Catholic, deeply resented the fact that after escaping from the Dominicans he had been converted to the evangelical faith, and prohibited him from speaking in any public place. As of old the issue was drawn, "Which is better to serve, God or man?"

In the meantime, Dr. Montano was making full proof of his ministry. Large numbers of the Indians in the mountains surrounding Cuzco were listening to his preaching. Now he understood the providential meaning of his Quechua Indian nurse and why she had been permitted to teach him in her native dialect the stories of the legendary heroes of her people, for he was able to preach to them in their own language.

At one point the Indians came in hundreds to the meetings. The authorities put quite a number of them in jail. Dr. Montano went to talk with the jailers. They said that the Indians had been made prisoners because they had not gone to work on the Catholic Church, as the priest had ordered. Dr. Montano, accustomed always to being obeyed, demanded that the doors be opened and the prisoners released. The jailers, accustomed always to obeying Dr. Montano's kind, opened the doors and permitted them their liberty. God wonderfully blessed the truth, and many of the Indians believed, as well as large numbers of the intellectuals and middle class, who also heard the Word gladly.

As Dr. Montano was extending his labours to an ever-widening circle of towns and cities, the leaders of the Dominican Order became convinced that persuasion could not be counted upon to stop him. In an effort to turn the people against him and incite them to violence against his person or instil such fear in them that they would refuse to listen, they began a preaching campaign in the Roman Catholic Churches against "the heretic". Upon a report which was submitted to the Vatican the sentence of excommunication issued by the Pope himself fell upon the gospel crusader, but Christ was too real to him for this to cause even a ripple of fear—he had found an experience which was beyond the reach of councils, prelates, or Colleges of Cardinals either to grant or to take from him.

Easter Week came soon in that first glad, joyous springtime of his fellowship with the living Son of God. It seemed strange perhaps, and yet faith always hopes for greater things than fear can ever deny. The Chapel Master of the Convent of Merced, for whom he had many times played Mass upon the organ and in whose musical programmes he had taken part, requested him to sing. Dr. Montano told him that he could do this only if he were permitted to make his own selections. Here was an opportunity to sing the gospel, and in the most unexpected place. Perhaps they were relenting. The songs chosen were "Jesu, Lover of My Soul" and "Divine Face of Christ".

On Monday of Holy Week the Dominican friars preached a sermon denouncing the heroic monk. As he was going to the railway station with Mr. Patton, accompanying two missionaries who were leaving for Bolivia, they met a representative of the Singer Sewing Machine Corporation whom Dr. Montano knew.

"What, are you still here?" he asked in amazement. "Do you not know of your danger? My wife is a friend of the wife of the Prefect. The authorities absolutely refuse to be responsible for your safety if you remain here. All is in readiness. They plan to do away with you today. Faithful Catholic Indians from many parts of the mountains are coming in for the procession of the 'Christ of the Earthquakes'. A great public demonstration against you is being organized. You will be sought and killed by the infuriated and drunken mob before sunset. You cannot stay here and live."

Mr. Patton saw at once the seriousness of the situation, how the net was being woven about Walter Manuel for his destruction. He immediately secured a good saddle-horse, and, against vigorous protests from his young convert, insisted on his leaving town at once in company with a trusted Christian. And so it was that he went into hiding for eight days, until the drunkenness and debauchery of the days of Holy Week should end and the aroused religious passion of the people somewhat abate.

Scarcely had he left the ranch where he had been secluded before he was informed by a lay member of the Dominican monastery that plenary indulgence had been promised to any-one who should kill the "renegade"—someone would be only too glad thus to ensure himself eternal life in the future and the favour of the Church now.

Not only had this general order been issued, but a young man had been definitely assigned, as a good and meritorious act, the task of assassinating the former priest. His friend from the monastery warned him to take every possible precaution.

Shortly after this chance meeting, returning home late one night from the mission in Cuzco, Dr. Montano had to pass through a dark street, unlighted save for the reflections from the two main thoroughfares between which this short, narrow passageway ran. Silhouetted against the brighter, far end of the street could be seen the outline of a man concerning whom he had been warned, who was standing still, waiting, arms held behind him. Dr. Montano might have turned and run, but he would not be a coward. He must go home. He claimed that God was protecting him. As he went forward in the darkness his heart felt a strange wonder, a lightness as though it had ceased to function for a moment. He could only pray as he went nearer, "O Christ, if this be Thy will, let Thy will be done!"

To the sinister, shadowy figure now so close to him he said as cordially as he could, "Good evening!"

As from a sepulchre a deep, hoarse voice answered, "Good evening!"

The hurrying feet of other passers-by could be heard coming down the street. Dr. Montano went on with even step, his back towards the would-be assassin. The other stood as though his hands were tied, watching, powerless to move. The Angel of the Lord is faithful still to those who trust Him.

But now was brought into action an influence which in Latin American countries is one of the strongest which may be invoked, the will, the command, the wishes of one's father. The age of the child has little to do in lessening parental authority. To disobey a father's desire is something that it is difficult for a child even to conceive.

A letter came from Dr. German Guillen Montano—"With tears flowing down my cheeks I beg of you to return to the monastery and ask for pardon."

A little later his father wrote another letter in still severer strain—"If you refuse to return to the Dominican monastery I will deny that you are my son and disinherit you!"

A third letter came—"Inasmuch as you have refused to return to the monastery, I am cutting you off as my son, and you have no further part as a member of our family." The "Kaiser" of Cochabamba University had spoken in terms which became the role he had always played.

It was night when Walter Manuel walked back from the post office with this letter. The Monastery of Santo Domingo loomed like a great black dot against the lighter background of the Andes, touched by the moon to trembling silver, and above the whiteness of their eternal snows the stars glowed brightly.

In his room at the simple mission home Fray Luis read and re-read his father's letter. He could do nothing but weep. His tears as they fell upon that page of bold, crisp Spanish writing blinded him until he could not see.

Facing him in his mission room and looking down upon him, as the smiling Virgin of the Rosary formerly had in his cell, was the well-known quotation, "Prayer changes things". In his heart the battle raged fiercely. So many times, with pressure from every side, poverty, affronts from authorities, slights and insults from former friends, a voice had told him that he was a fool. Now again that voice spoke with subtle insistence, "You *are* a fool! Your new friends will all play out on you! You will be left penniless, forsaken, living only to regret what you have thrown away! Friends, family, position, ease—it is all yours if you do not persist in this folly!"

"Prayer changes things!" The motto on the wall kept repeating itself over and over as he glanced up at it. He prayed that night. As formerly he said prayers, now, as the agony

G

of sorrow swept over his anguished soul, he prayed—prayed as Christ did at Gethsemane.

He talked with Mr. Patton, the missionary. "I will be your father here on earth," that good man assured him. Then later in God's Word he found, "When my father and my mother forsake me, then the Lord will take me up."

The next day he was able to reply courageously to his father's threat—"If you have denied me, still I have a Father who is in heaven. Not for anything that you have said or done can I deny the experience of peace and salvation which He has given to me and the joy that is mine."

CHAPTER FOURTEEN

THE NET IS SPREAD

Mᴏʀᴇ than ever Dr. Montano felt a love for his father. He knew that the stern old gentleman was suffering under the same religious deception which had bound his own heart for years. Gradually the conviction deepened that he should see him. Thus it was that the decision was made to visit the scenes of his childhood.

His father's absence at the depot when he arrived in Cochabamba after a seven-years' absence could mean nothing less than intentional insult. One of the family maids was at the station, and highly as he regarded these servants who in other days had cared for him, none the less it increased his awareness of the gulf which now separated him from home.

Rebuffed thus by his own family in the first moments of his arrival, he turned at once towards the Baptist mission station, where Rev. Mr. Hillyer, who had read of his conversion in Press notices and religious periodicals, welcomed him most graciously.

Next morning he battled with himself as to whether he should call upon the family. Having been thus insulted at the hour of his arrival, what could he expect? Was there any way that he could be a blessing to his father, or help him to understand the new life which he had discovered in Christ Jesus? But at last he set out, walking alone towards the beautiful, aristocratic suburbs of the city.

He had not gone far when he saw his father walking towards him with the baston or walking-stick of a Doctor of Laws in his hand. In a moment he forgot all the differences between them; that he was no longer a son but had been disinherited for bringing disgrace upon the family name. With the impulsive love of his boyhood days he stretched out his arms and started towards his father to embrace him. The "Kaiser", as though his son's very presence was defiling, raised a hand warningly to indicate that he should keep his distance. However, the older man permitted Walter Manuel to walk on towards the house with him. Once inside, he was scarcely offered a seat.

A moment after entering the large living-room his step-mother returned from Mass. He rose and stepped towards her, bowing with deep respect and extending his hand. She ignored his words and his presence.

"Alta Gracia!" ordered the "Kaiser", speaking her name; "at least answer the greeting!"

Her reply was silence.

"I will be leaving at once," said his son, taking up his hat and stick.

His father walked silently and sadly with him to the door, and without saying a word, accompanied him down the street as though to give him this courtesy in bidding him good-bye.

All at once the father became a little more genial. "I will walk with you a bit," he said.

Together they went on down San Juan de Dios Avenue and, guided by the older man, turned into Baptista Street, named in honour of Dr. Montano's uncle, a former President of Bolivia. He noticed they were approaching the Bishop's palace, and in a moment his father had turned into the grounds and they were walking towards the front entrance.

Some plan had evidently been arranged. Just what pressure would be exerted, what inducement or threat to cause him to desist from following Christ, he could not know.

The outside door opened and they found themselves standing in a waiting-room. Almost at once they were ushered into the great audience-room of the Catholic prelate, who was standing in his purple bishop's robes behind a large oaken table. Before him was a document which he passed towards the young man as he approached. "All you need to do, Fray Luis, is to sign this," he said with finality.

Dr. Montano looked from the Bishop's cordial smile to the paper which he was supposed to sign, and began to read, "I, Fray Luis Montano, beg to be forgiven of my sin in having become a Protestant and of having embraced the heretical doctrines of Luther, and I promise to return to the Holy Roman Catholic Church, and I accept the professorship in Latin at the Apostolic Roman Catholic Seminary and a position in the Cathedral of Cochabamba."

Here were honours, money, the favour of great and small, the kindness of former friends restored, his father's love, all that culture and wealth can bring to ensure happiness in this life—all this for a signature which would take him thirty seconds to write. But was that all? He hesitated.

"Look at your father," said the Bishop dramatically. "See, he is weeping; you are refusing his love, you are breaking his heart. Sign this as a good son of the Holy Mother Church and you will bring joy to his soul and to yourself such favours as perhaps none who has been guilty of your sins has ever been offered."

Walter Manuel turned and saw his father shaken by sobs— *his* father, the "Kaiser", whom no one had ever seen shed a tear.

The old gentleman came closer to his son, staggeringly, almost falling, and putting up his hands he leaned upon him as upon the only stay of his advancing age and, trembling with emotion, said pleadingly in tones of deepest love and affection, "You, you are at least my son. You cannot, you cannot deny me this. You must sign it. You, you shall return to your home and to your Church. You shall be honoured in this town. The Church is very lenient with you. They have done what they could, because you are a son of German Guillen Montano. You cannot, tell them, tell me, 'No!' "

For a moment Dr. Montano seemed swayed irresistibly towards a favourable decision. Centuries of feudal chivalry, a life-long exposure to a society where "No" was never spoken; blood, culture, spirit, reason—all seemed bending him to an inevitable acquiescence.

There could be but one answer humanly. His response was as fixed as the course of the stars.

But suddenly the morning of January 3rd flashed upon the screen of his mind. It was 10.30 a.m. He was rising to his feet, his face still wet with the tears of penitence, his heart filled with new-found peace and joy.

As though a fresh breeze had struck him, his flagging purpose revived. He straightened up. The time for action had come. Slowly and as clearly as possible he gave his testimony —the seven years of monastic life, the penances which he had endured, the long vigils before the Virgin of the Rosary, the growing unrest and desperation of his heart, the atheism into which he had finally plunged as a result of the deceptions of the Church, then, glorious spiritual dawn, peace, joy, salvation, the presence of the living Christ.

When he had finished the Bishop picked up the paper coldly and turned away as he said to the father, "It is useless to talk more concerning this."

Slowly, with faltering step, refusing any assistance, the older man walked from the room, down the steps, and to the pavement, where father and son parted in silence, each going his own way.

Despite the ache he felt in his heart at saddening a beloved father, there was joy—joy in the midst of tears which he could not restrain, joy, though he must seem an ingrate son, and home and family and worldly honour were thus lost to him for ever. And no wonder, for a greater victory than he knew had been wrought that morning through the blood of the Lamb and the word of his testimony. Later this Bishop Garret returned to Rome, relinquished to the Vatican his robes, his ring, and all insignia of office, renounced his Catholic faith, and is today a preacher of the gospel in Latin America.

If such had been Dr. Montano's reception in his home, he felt that Candelaria Rodriguez Montano, a greatly-beloved cousin, would understand. When that afternoon he arrived at the girl's home, Candelaria herself answered his knock. She had always been more like a sister to him than a cousin. She paused, surprised by his presence, then, without speaking a word, but with a look of intense scorn, bent close enough to spit in his face, and slammed the door.

He turned towards the home of Eliodoro Villazon, former President of Bolivia. This great and good man had frequently taken Walter Manuel upon his knees as a boy and talked with him of dreams for his future, and when the lad had decided upon a Church career had reluctantly contented himself with the thought that he would at least become Bishop of Cochabamba. When one of the two daughters with whom Eliodoro Villazon lived answered the door she called out the news of Walter Manuel's presence. A voice spoke out angrily, ordering the door to be closed at once. Disheartened, wounded, wondering, the young man turned in bewilderment towards the home of the missionaries, Mr. and Mrs. Hillyer, scarcely believing that what he had experienced was real.

On May 28th a great birthday party was held in honour of German Guillen Montano. He had recently been appointed Judge of Cochabamba and was celebrating the completion of twenty-five years of service as Professor, Director, and Regent of Education of the State, and at one time he had also served as first judge of the capital of the republic. Friends from every walk of life came to pay their respects. There were Indian chiefs in their curious costumes, middle-class people, as well as the intellectuals and those of the aristocracy. The school and governmental authorities and employees turned out *en masse*. Floral tributes were seen in profusion throughout the house. All pressed towards the honoured man as they entered to express their congratulations and good wishes for the future.

In the evening there was an official banquet. Several times during the meal someone insisted that Walter Manuel drink a toast of wine to his father, but he had refused. Only those who know the Latins' insistence upon conformity to the social amenities, and how terrible a thing it is ever to refuse what is "proper", can understand his suffering and what courage his refusal demanded. Dr. Montano called upon all his social arts in declining so that he might wound as little as possible the sensibilities of those who could not understand. He had requested soda-water and thus had drunk his father's health.

As they left the banquet hall and passed out into the large living-room for dancing and drinking, one young lady after another, sometimes mockingly, sometimes in friendly interest, came to insist upon his dancing. Again he must do what no good Latin ever does, say "No." A bevy of girls came and, holding their wine-glasses before him, invited him publicly to drink to his father's health. He pushed away the glass of wine and asked for soda-water. The father was so exasperated that he strode over to his son and demanded, "What do you mean by these actions? Have you come to ruin our feast?"

Dr. Montano, as graciously as he could, replied, "No, Father. I am very sorry indeed to cause you this trouble. I have not come for that purpose, but only to show you that I still love you."

"Oh, these Protestants, these *Protestants*!" lamented the father, his anger turning to pity and sorrow with the kindly words his son had spoken. "They are destroying the soul of my Walter, poor lad!"

There seemed nothing for Dr. Montano now but to leave. He called a servant and asked for his hat and stick. As he stood at the door to bow good evening to the company the troubled father came up to him. "My son, forgive me. You have acted terribly, of course, but please forget it, and forgive me, my son."

"But the place where I sleep closes early. I must be leaving if I am to stay there tonight."

His father reached down and took the young man's stick and hat with a touch of that familiar authority which a son loves in a parent, as he said, "You stay here tonight. I will say nothing more to you."

At one o'clock in the morning the long day of celebration ended.

There was still one more step open to those who wished to save Dr. Montano from the malevolent influence of the Protestants—coercion. And this was now attempted.

According to the law of Bolivia all young men must serve in the army. At the age when ordinarily Walter Manuel would have been in training he had gone to the monastery and, as priests are exempt from military duty, he had not been called. Now that he had renounced the Dominican Order he ceased to be a priest and therefore could technically be considered as not having fulfilled his obligation to his country.

The situation was indeed a serious one. As Dr. Montano well knew, there were distant jungle regions where the worst criminals and deserters from the army were deported and where, never heard from again, the vast tropics seemed to have swallowed them completely. With the hatred of the Church which had such intimately confidential relations with the Government and the desertion of his own politically-powerful family, it could easily be that, unless God delivered him, the threat of deportation would become a reality.

One day his father threatened angrily as they met, "If you will not return to the Church, then I will turn you over to the State as one who has illegally avoided army service. There can be no escape for you."

"This would be a terrible punishment indeed," answered Walter Manuel evenly. "But should I have to spend all my life in the terrible region of Acre or El Beni among the shameful criminals of that land, not even for this could I leave Christ

Jesus or return to the Roman Church which has deceived me so long. No, a thousand times would I rather serve as a soldier or a prisoner than leave the peace and salvation which now are mine."

The Baptist Mission of Cochabamba had arranged with Dr. Montano for a series of public services. One of his uncles, then a deputy and at this time Mayor of Cochabamba, called personally to interview his nephew. "Son," he pleaded with the young man, "there are certainly some depths to which you will not descend. Now that you have brought this terrible blot upon the family name, surely you will not preach anything of your new faith here where everyone knows you and us. You would not wish us to suffer such shame, would you?"

After discussing the matter with the missionaries it was felt that to continue might seem like studied insult and arouse such fury of resistance as to make more difficult the preaching of the gospel in the future, and even threaten the existence of the mission. The dates were cancelled.

Every familiar door had closed. Every former friend had turned against him. There was not one of that intimate circle of which he had once been a leading member who treated him with anything except bitter, fanatical hatred or studied attempts to swerve him from the Via Dolorosa which leads to Calvary, and which, bearing his cross, he determined to follow, cost what it might. Fruitless though it seemed, he had still obeyed the Voice in being a witness "in Jerusalem".

He had seen his father's face for the last time. Accompanied only by his friends of the Protestant mission, Walter Manuel sadly, secretly, took the morning train. He watched his home fade into the purple haze of the distance with that inward sickness of heart of one losing the last natural tie which binds him to the past.

The snow-crowned Andes towered above him in dazzling beauty and purity, cut sharp against the blue depths of the sky. They spoke to Walter Manuel of that eternal kingdom which could not be shaken by the passing storms of the lower levels. They seemed to him like the hills of God's own glorious Zion whence might come strength and courage for the fight which lay ahead.

CHAPTER FIFTEEN

OVER THE DAMASCUS WALL

S T. PAUL, writing to the Corinthian Christians, could say, "Wherever I go, thank God, He makes my life a constant pageant of triumph." Nevertheless there was a time when he needed to be secretly spirited away to protect him from those who sought his life—even a Roman prison could serve the divine purposes. Such testings have come to many in the history of the Church of God.

Dr. Montano returned from Cochabamba without position, plan, or purpose except to follow Christ. He was fleeing from his home and family, an outcast, a nobody, his only possessions peace and salvation, his doctor's baston and his English spats. His brother, a physician of liberal tendencies, destined later to die in the service of his country in the Gran Chaco War, received him into his home at La Paz, the capital of Bolivia.

Here Dr. Montano learned that President Siles, a close friend of his brother's family, had, only a short time before, succeeded in stamping out a communistic revolution. It was but natural that he should send a letter of congratulation. A very cordial acknowledgment signed by the President was received.

A few days later, after having been cross-examined by a Government detective, Dr. Montano was called to appear before the Prefect or President of the district. This man was a very fanatical Catholic. The ex-priest found himself accused by the bishop of being leader of the dangerous communistic group which had so recently attempted to destroy the existing Government. "As a result of this," he was informed, "you must be deported from the country."

The accused man drew from his pocket President Siles' letter. "Will you please, for just a moment, compare this letter with the accusations which you have before you?" he requested. Allowing time for the letter to be read, he witnessed boldly for the Christ who had given him peace, salvation, and continuous spiritual victory.

As the Prefect looked from the shining, earnest face of the

younger man to the President's letter which lay before him, he picked up the bishop's accusations and tore them to shreds as he said, "What rascally, perverse friars these fellows are!" And then added, "As for you, Dr. Montano, you may stay here as long as you will, with the fullest liberty, and if anything happens to you please inform me at once."

A few weeks later another Government detective appeared. "There is no need for your working with these Protestants," he urged. "You can just as well be working for the Government. The Secretary of Foreign Relations will make you subsecretary. Instead of this Protestant business why do you not accept such an offer? You will be second to him in the department and receive a very good salary with prestige."

To a member of his family, Government work, with its prestige and authority, was as the very bread of life. The enemy had indeed found a naturally weak point in his defence. While the force of such an appeal must have been very great, with its offered money and influence and the opportunity to continue his present beliefs, still only one answer was possible if he were to obey "the Voice".

"It is true," replied Dr. Montano, "that I do not now receive a salary from anyone, but I do have a piece of bread to eat each day. I am happy: I am doing the will of God. I cannot accept the offer."

Later he learned that prominent Catholic leaders had agreed, "We cannot do anything against him by force or persecution, but let us offer him a good position in the Government, and this will take his time and energy, and gradually he will cease to be a Protestant." The ruse had failed. He continued his services in the La Paz Baptist Church.

But real adventure, almost tragedy, awaited him at Puno, on the other side of Lake Titicaca, as he resumed his journey back to Cuzco. Here, as he stood in the hotel lobby waiting for breakfast, two police detectives dressed as country fellows came in asking for Dr. Montano. As his name was called he left the side of a fellow-passenger, a Mrs. McConnel, with whom he was conversing, and placed himself at their orders.

"The Prefect wishes to talk with you at once," they informed him.

"This is very strange," remarked Dr. Montano as he started off with them.

Stranger still was the fact that he was not being taken to the Government buildings, but to the city jail. Here the Chief of Police very abruptly relieved him of all his papers and personal belongings.

"Why, what has happened?" asked Dr. Montano in bewilderment.

"You will see, you will see!" was the only answer.

When the preliminary personal examination had been completed the policemen were called. "Put him in *that* place," was the enigmatic order.

The policemen roughly shoved Dr. Montano ahead of them down into the lower part of the jail, and in a semi-underground passage-way he was violently forced into a dark hole which could not be dignified with the name room. It was about three by four feet around the walls, and about six feet high. There were no windows, no light, no ventilation. In the utter darkness he was conscious of the unspeakable filth upon the damp floor, and a stifling odour made his senses reel. There was not even a crack through which fresh air could enter. He felt that a short time here would mean death.

Like a film rapidly unfolding before his mind he saw the past, the mobs, the slights of friends, the loss of family, the repeated efforts of his father to dissuade him from his faith, the bitter, unending persecution. In anguish he cried out, "O God! what can it be? Are these things the result of my wrong choice? Surely if I were in Thy will these things would not happen to me. Am I suffering all this because I escaped from the monastery? If you desire that I should return, tell me clearly and I will do it. I wish only to obey Thee. Guide me plainly. I will do anything that is Thy will. But why must I suffer this? Deliver me, O Lord!"

Dr. Montano was not given to visions. But while he stood there, reeling from the stench of the dungeon filth, it seemed to him all at once as though a light began to shine through the spiritual and mental darkness—that a strange radiance filled the place. Then in an instant he could see the face of Christ, as close and real as that of a beloved friend. The crown of thorns was upon His brow, and yet in the midst of the anguish of His passion He was smiling, smiling approval and encouragement, smiling as one who, hanging from Calvary's Cross, could think first of others. His arms were outstretched, crucified, His hands so near that Walter Manuel might have reached out and touched the bleeding palms. And then, dropping before that vision of the Christ, beautiful in agony, shining with triumphant love, he cried out, "O Lord! Forgive me for ever questioning Thee!" And then repeated, knowing that Christ would understand, "Lord, I am ready! I am ready!"

Yes, now he was ready indeed—ready to live, if life were granted to him, ready to die if that hour had come, ready to serve without complaint, ready to go forward without ever again thinking of finding an easier way. At last he had come to that deeper understanding of Calvary, vainly sought in the monastery. For the first time the reality of the price paid for his redemption gripped his heart. He had seen on the Cross the face of a Friend, the face of a Man who died for him, the face of his Christ. Life could never be the same again.

A few moments later the door of the dungeon opened and the Chief of Police ordered, "Follow me!" As his eyes became accustomed to the light in the room into which he was led he saw the Bolivian Consul and Mrs. McConnel standing to receive him. This kind-hearted Peruvian lady had seen the two detectives lead him away from the hotel lobby, and as she knew of another Bolivian who had been arrested and subjected to terrible tortures in this same jail, when he did not return, she feared for his safety. She had hurried to the Consul, who at once demanded the release of the prisoner and offered his personal guarantee to the authorities.

"But we cannot release him," answered the Chief of Police. "We are responsible for him. We have orders from the Prefect of Cuzco to send him directly there."

The Consul replied indignantly, "But I cannot permit him to remain in that dungeon. Such a course on your part as a representative of Peru will be considered an unfriendly act to my country, and I will start diplomatic action at once."

The Puno police officers in a more conciliatory tone apologized, stating, "We are not interested in keeping him in jail, but we have a telegram which we must obey."

There was nothing more to do. Dr. Montano thanked the Consul and Mrs. McConnel for their services on his behalf and was led away to one of the larger rooms in the jail. While a great improvement over the dungeon, it was little better than a torture-room. Part of the floor was cement, the remainder dirt. Here were herded together a conglomerate group of criminals, drunkards, beggars, and insane. The corners of the room were indescribably filthy. Lice were crawling on the men's clothing. The antics of some of the demented ones, thrown in indiscriminately with the others, were horrible.

Meal-time came. He was given neither a glass of water nor a crust of bread. Meals were not served in this section, but prisoners were dependent upon family or friends to supply their needs. Most of the men received meals from those on the outside who had not forgotten. One beggar covered with lice and filth offered kindly to share his lunch with Dr. Montano. He would like to have eaten as an act of friendliness, but the situation was so utterly revolting that he found it necessary to decline food on such terms as these.

The days and nights alike were a slowly-moving nightmare. Some of the men would be crying, others cursing or calling vile epithets at the authorities. Dr. Montano remembered the vision of the Christ which had come to him in the dungeon and preached to them of a Saviour. When the guards came he would also witness to them of the living Christ with power to transform the heart. Secretly the police after the first day were striving to show him some kindness, but they could not very well do this, as orders came from the superiors that no favours were to be shown Fray Luis.

At times the guards would ask him, "What is the difference between you and these others? Why are you not crying out, cursing and demanding to see the sun, and asking for water and food?"

As Dr. Montano told them the story of what made this difference he had the joy of receiving the promise from some of these rough men that they would give their hearts to God. Thus, right in prison, an "effectual door" was opened for testifying concerning Christ Jesus, the Lord, and the peace and salvation which He brings to the fully-surrendered heart.

After three days and nights of this veritable inferno a group of soldiers appeared fully armed with rifles and pistols. He was taken from the prison room, surrounded by the soldiers, and marched to the railroad station. He was ordered to sit down in the waiting-room while a soldier with fixed bayonet stood on guard before him.

Dr. Montano was still a human being. Shame swept over

him as he sat there with a curious crowd milling about, craning their necks to catch sight of what they must have regarded as a dangerous criminal. It had been impossible for him to keep clean, and his appearance was such that this alone was most humiliating. There was the possibility that at any moment some intimate friend might see him.

A little later, under the soldiers' orders, he entered one of the coaches. With all the suffering he sensed a deep calm. God had known he would need courage and strength for the days immediately ahead and so had permitted him to be thrust into the dungeon darkness where the vision came which now buoyed him up and for ever cut off all thought of retreat.

After about four hours of travel in the coach the soldier who was standing guard over him relaxed a bit and began to talk with him. "All that you are going through must be very hard," he said. "But I see I can trust you."

Dr. Montano again told the story of how he had found peace and salvation, and of the joy and strength which had come to him with the vision of his crucified Lord.

"Well, this is what I think," answered the soldier, "and others there in the jail said the same thing—the priests are attacking you without reason and attempting to make you a martyr because you have become a Protestant. But you are a good man, I know that."

The soldier took down his gun and removed the bayonet. "If you will give me your word of honour I will leave you alone, for I know that I can trust you." The guard put his bayonet into its case and went into the other end of the coach.

A little later an old grey-haired man who had been one of Walter Manuel's teachers, now the Prior of three monasteries, entered the car. He manifested astonishment at finding his former pupil in so unkempt a condition and sat down beside him.

"Where are you going? What can have happened?" the Prior asked.

"Had you come a little sooner," replied Dr. Montano, "you would have seen that soldier yonder standing over me with fixed bayonet, as though I were a murderer."

"But what have you done?" the Prior inquired.

"That is just it," returned Walter Manuel. "What *have* I done? Is it because the priests are ordering this persecution?"

"Well," responded the Prior warily, "many of them are doing things against my will. A group of priests was called together in Arequipa in order to secure the papal excommunication. I told them, 'You have no proof against him.' But so many opposed you that there was nothing that I could do."

It was night when the train bearing Dr. Montano and his guard arrived in Cuzco. Only a short time before he had resided here in one of the proudest monasteries of the new world. Every need, want, or fancy had been supplied. He had time for writing, study, friends. He had renown in the Press. The future was bright, with every prospect of a brilliant career. He had everything except peace and salvation, and he found that without these there were not enough other things to satisfy his soul.

The missionaries of the city immediately rallied to his support, and secured three lawyers to defend his case in court, though it could have been foretold from the first that, whatever the evidence, the decision would be unfavourable. The principal charge against Dr. Montano was that inasmuch as the nation recognized and protected the Apostolic Roman Catholic Religion, therefore in becoming a Protestant and in preaching contrary to the doctrines of the Catholic Church he was in effect preaching against the Government; or, in other words, had become guilty of treason. The prosecuting attorney demanded that he be deported to the farthest jungles of Peru, whence it would be certain that he could never return. Mr. Patton, who covered the trial for the religious Presses of South America, wrote, "As the Jews cried out concerning Christ before Pilate, so it is here, 'If thou let this man go, thou art not Caesar's friend!' " The jailers took advantage of every opportunity to heap indignities upon the prisoner.

At last the trial was ended. Dr. Montano was pronounced guilty and sentenced to deportation. He was to be sent in disgrace from the land in which his family during a hundred years and more had been so influential. He was being treated as a dangerous criminal because he had cared to accept by simple faith God's wonderful gift of salvation through the blood of Jesus Christ his Lord and to be a witness for his Redeemer.

The night before the deportation Mr. Patton came and spent the evening with him in his jail cell. Sunny, big-hearted, devoted, spiritual, full of youth and youth's devotion to Christ, he was God's own messenger to the prisoner. The next morning it was discovered that an officer of comparatively high rank in the army was to accompany Dr. Montano, so the missionaries, fearing that this might mean some sort of foul play, sought and obtained permission for Mr. Patton to accompany him.

The second morning after their departure the party arrived at Lake Titicaca, whose sleepy depths hold the mystery of the past civilizations whose ruins abound upon its shores. The officer here delivered Dr. Montano into the hands of a steamship captain. "My duty ends here," he said. "Watch him that he does not climb off the boat until he is across the line of Bolivia." So after all he was not being deported into the terrible life of the jungle.

Mr. Patton took leave of the younger man as a father of his son. They waved to each other as the ship slipped from the wharf and started towards Bolivia. Little did they know that only once more would they see each other on earth. Perhaps the great task for which God had sent Mr. Patton to South America had now been accomplished.

In La Paz, Dr. Montano spent two months preaching daily in the Baptist Church. His message was beginning to make a deep impression on thinking people. His social position, his unique experiences, the firmness with which he had resisted every effort to destroy him were capturing the imagination of the public. If the entire Catholic Church and its entrenched ecclesiastics, with the power of the Government behind them, could not silence this lone prophetic voice which cried out in the spiritual wilderness, it was little wonder that Press and public alike should be captivated by the sheer audacity of the man.

On June 23rd, 1927, none other than Dr. Alberto Ostria Gutierrez called Dr. Montano to the editorial offices of *La Prensa*, one of the outstanding papers of South America, and after interviewing him minutely relative to his religious experience, wrote a leading article over his own name which was copied throughout the Press of South America. Dr. Montano found that his articles were again in demand, and thus he was enabled to preach with his pen more widely than would ever have been possible but for his fruitless search for God in the

H

Dominican monastery and the persecutions which followed his escape.

The excitement was increasing. The determination of the clergy to destroy this new menace to their rule was bound to find other ways of achieving its object. The persecution in La Paz grew in intensity as the Baptist church was crowded night after night. The threatening murmur became an unmistakable roar. All were convinced that he would certainly be killed if he remained.

As prayer was being offered by the church concerning Dr. Montano's future, a letter came from Dr. Harry Strachan, president of the well-known Bible Institute of Costa Rica, offering a place of refuge until doors should again open in South America. So it was, with a consciousness of being in the divine will, that Walter Manuel left La Paz and started his journey towards voluntary exile in a distant land.

When at last he landed at Puerto Limon, Costa Rica, a telegram of welcome from Dr. and Mrs. Strachan and the faculty of the Bible school was awaiting him. A day later he arrived by train at San Jose, Costa Rica, where he was greeted by the missionaries, who conducted him to the Institute. Here he was given a reception by the teachers and students, among them a young American lady who had not been at the station to greet him, Miss Esther Piper, whose beautiful singing was an outstanding feature of the evening.

Thus did Dr. Montano escape over his "Damascus Wall" to have "three years in Arabia" in the seclusion of the Costa Rica Bible Institute, where he became grounded in Protestant theology and practice while also serving as a teacher and—but that is another story!

CHAPTER SIXTEEN

THE VIRGIN'S RIVAL

Miss Esther Piper was a dark-eyed young woman, beautiful with the warm, rosy colouring which perfect health bestows. Gifted with a voice of surprising range and power, she became at an early age an outstanding music pupil. Her father, Rev. William Hammer Piper, was for years the devoted pastor of the Interdenominational Stone Church of Chicago, and her mother served joyfully at his side. With such a background it was but natural that she entered Moody Bible Institute in preparation for service as an evangelist.

Soon, however, an enthusiastic vocal teacher urged Miss Piper to give herself to concert work, and some even suggested the operatic stage as the proper sphere for her unusual voice and her radiant personality. But God's vision held. Soul-winning was His first call, and all else given to her was merely a trust to be used as He wished.

When Leon Tucker organized a world evangelistic party, Miss Piper was elected as singer. While the work with Dr. and Mrs. Tucker and their fine corps of workers was most interesting, down in her heart of hearts was the conviction that God would some day send her forth as a missionary. Friends argued that she was already a missionary and that by singing the gospel in various countries she could reach many hearts. She felt God urging something more than this. So she went back to Moody and enrolled in the course for missionaries.

There were those who were ready to tell her the decision was foolish—that she would be wasting her talents on a mission-field. And, let it be admitted, so real was the temptation, so speciously convincing were the arguments, that at times a very real battle raged as the love of music clashed with the loving call of her Christ; but He always won and held her steady to the purpose which had burned in her heart from girlhood. The fight had been won in long nights of prayer; and yet, like so many of life's battles, it was a victory which needed to be made effective daily by continuous triumph. The real crisis came during a vacation period at home. Her mother,

as young and attractive in the beauty of her Christian womanhood as one of her own daughters, knew, as mothers usually
seem to know, of the battle going on in Esther's heart, and
without saying much helped greatly.

One day as the family was gathered about the piano Esther
began singing "Yielded". In that moment God showed her
that the last thing needed was an utter, entire, unswerving
yielding of her full will to Him. Her heart was so flooded with
a sense of the presence of God's Spirit that the singing had to
stop and all knelt together around the piano; and there it was
that a deeper consecration than she had ever known before
was made and she felt her soul flooded with peace and joy in
the assurance of full and final surrender to all the will of God.

Upon her return to Moody she turned with all her energy
to missionary preparation. While the Institute had various
missionary prayer bands, including China, Japan, India,
Africa, and others, in some mysterious way which caused even
her to marvel, Miss Piper felt herself being drawn towards the
Latin-American missionary group. A week before graduation
she was privileged to meet Mrs. Strachan, wife of the president
of the Costa Rica Bible Institute. At once they were drawn to
each other. A long interview and prayer time followed. Mrs.
Strachan felt definitely that this beautiful and talented young
woman should go to Latin America. The assurance at last came
to her that this was God's will for her yielded life and heart.

But friends still clung to her, whispering of concert work.
She was a member of the various musical organizations of the
great city of Chicago. Every door opened before her, but down
in her heart she still said, "My heart, O God, is fixed to do
Thy will." And three weeks after graduation Esther Piper was
on her way to Central America.

She hardly knew why, as she bade goodbye to her young
friends, as she kissed her mother, it might be for the last time,
tears, floods of tears, welled up out of the depths of her very
soul. If for a moment she had desired the world she was leaving, a nod of her head and it was hers. But she did not want it.
She wanted God's will. And God's will was Central America.

All the way to New Orleans, where she took the boat, the
tears flowed. And yet, strange paradox of the walk with God,
there was a deep settled peace which nothing could disturb, the
sweet assurance of obeying God, which, after all, is greater

joy than the world, even at its best, ever knows in the moments of its fleeting jollity.

The boat on which Esther embarked was the finest. Mrs. Strachan and her daughter, due to illness, had to be quarantined in their cabin. This left the young missionary to mingle with the other passengers. Among them was a leading manufacturer of the United States, his wife, and a party of friends. They were nominal Christians. They took a deep interest in Miss Piper. Everyone was kind to her. The sense of loneliness was vanishing. In the intimate circle of life on shipboard, where the formalities are so largely relaxed, she told them of her purpose in going to Central America. Here before this company of the elite her witnessing began. To them it seemed strange, inexplicable, that she, beautiful, full of life, with seemingly every prospect before her which beauty and culture open to a young person, planned to bury herself alive down in the tropics. A missionary!

Then they heard her sing. That settled it. They must save this impressionable young lady from the delusions which possessed her! It was utter foolishness for her to think of being a missionary. Why waste herself utterly and receive nothing? She would be unappreciated. These people did not want the gospel. The task of missions was a futile one. The whole thought of going down to save Latin America was just a bit of youthful presumption from which they would rescue her. The group of new-found friends, among whom was the Consul of Peru, banded together and raised money for all expenses of the return trip so that she might escape the consequences of what, to them, was an adolescent religious impulse misguided into devotion to Missions.

Here was a different kind of battle from what she had expected, waged by professing Christians of culture and refinement who knew the world and who knew Latin America and told her that the call of God upon her heart was a wild, unpractical dream, born of youthful enthusiasm. Mrs. Strachan was quarantined in her cabin. She had to fight, humanly, alone.

When the vessel reached Costa Rica there was no doubt in her mind as to God's will. She still felt homesickness and tears still welled up from deep within her heart. Sometimes, she hardly knew why, she cried herself to sleep at night. But what did that matter when she knew, *knew*, that Jesus was guiding her definitely into the life work that He had chosen for her?

When the girls of the Institute first caught sight of her dark hair and brown eyes they cried, "She is one of us! She is one of us!" and grabbed her and carried her off with that abandonment which only those of southern lands know. The missionaries were very glad to see her. As they knelt together she was too much overcome to pray aloud, but all seemed to understand. At Chicago, as the train had pulled out, the students from Moody had been singing, "God Be with You Till We Meet Again". Now she found the Costa Ricans singing this song in Spanish at nearly every service. No wonder the tears were so much of the time very near the surface.

Almost immediately God began to use the yielded vessel. To the Latin, music is the universal language, and a musician has an open sesame to his heart. Trusting the Holy Spirit to guide, the first classes were begun in a cappella chorus, harmony, and voice. She attempted beforehand to study out the words and phrases which she would need in the class. The students helped her, acting as interpreters, both of the language and the people. Joy gradually began to take the place of the unbidden sadness which had overshadowed her. Of course there were some laughable errors, as when she called a gentleman "caballo", which is "horse", instead of "caballero" or "knight", which is the Spanish word "sir". Neither could she keep "exhale" and "inhale" straightened out. Never more than a sly twinkle in the eyes of her pupils, however, disclosed a mistake, for Latin politeness made it impossible for them to think of laughing at the foibles of the visitors.

Even missionaries enjoy having friends. While entirely faithful to the call of God, she appreciated the social contacts with families on the large, near-by country estates where her beautiful voice gave her entrée. They taught her to ride horseback in the intervals of the grind of teaching, and thereby death made the first attempt to end her career as a missionary.

At Atenas, a little town of the district, she had been given a very unmanageable mount. The young man who was supposed to be in charge of the horses was half drunk. No sooner was she in the saddle than her horse started to run away. The drunken lad, mistaking for mere joy in a gallop what was to her a desperately dangerous moment, came speeding behind

her adding to the wild running of her horse by crying
"Bravo!" and swinging his hat. Esther felt herself slipping
from the saddle. She looked back at the galloping, half-
drunken Costa Rica stable-boy, as though pleading for help,
and then fell rolling to the ground. The scars of those wounds
and the tenderness of bruised or exposed nerves she will carry
with her until the day of her death.

Here at the Bible Institute of Costa Rica, under the direction
of President Harry Strachan, working in co-operation with the
Latin-American Evangelization Campaign, she laboured as
one of eight teachers doing intensive work with the twenty-
five boarding students, selected from the best in various
countries of South America.

When word was received of the intense and bitter persecution which Dr. Montano had been undergoing, Dr. Strachan,
with the thought, perhaps, of saving his life and giving him
the much-needed opportunity to consolidate his spiritual gains,
sent a cablegram to the young converted priest, asking him
to find at the Institute a refuge from his enemies. When he
arrived, Miss Piper, she scarcely knew why, did not go to the
station to welcome him—just a woman's reason.

That evening after dinner she went into the living-room to
improvise at the piano and sing for her own amusement.
Before long one of the teachers asked the privilege of intro-
ducing Dr. Montano. So it was for the first time that she met
Fray Luis, the former Dominican monk. He appeared to her
as a rather forlorn, tired but friendly young man who bore the
marks of much suffering. She at once noted the sacerdotal
severity of the countenance, the stern seriousness of earnest
youth, the questioning yet insistent eyes which asked for, in
fact, demanded truth, softened, however, by that strange
warmth which is characteristic of the child of God.

"Sing for me, please," Dr. Montano asked. Later someone
suggested that he join Miss Piper in a duet.

The Institute buzzed with the adventures of Dr. Montano.
He taught certain courses and studied Protestant theology. As
for paying any special attention to Miss Piper, that was impossible. Etiquette, race, language, family, all that and more
made it unthinkable that he should aspire to her hand.

Dr. Montano reached Costa Rica in September 1927. In
December of the same year, Mrs. Lydia M. Piper came to see

her daughter. She met Dr. Montano and, as a mother of her years has a right to do, fell in love with him. As for the daughter, she liked the young ex-monk, but love—that was another matter altogether. If race and grace, if lineage and culture and individual work count at all, they all counted heavily in the young man's favour. But in the States and also in Costa Rica there had not been lacking young men who proposed that she share their life. But she had only smiled as she shook her head and wondered what it was which made them seem so excited and do such queer things.

Walter Manuel called to see the mother and stayed to talk with Esther. He had never before known a mother's love, for his own had died when he was three years of age. Mrs. Piper was good and kind and faithful to him as a spiritual guide and counsellor. She became also a willing chaperon for her daughter.

Others finally noticed the young man's interest in the music teacher. For him, here was an ideal made flesh and blood. He had often wondered what fellowship with pure and perfect womanhood might be. Well, here he was experiencing it. He could never have interpreted his feelings as love—that would have frightened him. It was something much more abstract than that, more like poetry or art. In her presence he felt as though he was standing before a sublime picture. Her words seemed those of some religious oracle.

Yet, as though to prove once more that out of the greatest evils may come the greatest good, it was only when death itself struck again that his love was awakened.

CHAPTER SEVENTEEN

THE ROMANCE OF A MONK

DURING the summer vacation of 1928 Mrs. Piper and her daughter went to a friend's home in Puntarenas, which fronted on the ocean, about one hundred miles from the Institute. Here they had their farewell days together before the mother returned to her home in the North. A beautiful tropical beach was theirs alone. Each morning they enjoyed the sun, took a dip in the waves, or lay in the shade talking over the past or musing about the future.

One morning Miss Piper had scarcely entered the warm waters when her mother heard a terrible scream. A savage stingaree, such as are found in the tropics, had thrust his tail through the younger woman's foot just below the instep. Agonized by the pain and calling wildly for help, she came back out of the water. About an inch of flesh had been torn away. The blood was gushing from the wound in a torrent. She felt her strength going. Deep in the foot the poison was already paining greatly. Her mother had no knowledge of what to do in such an emergency as this and ran with the hope of finding some neighbour woman.

Just then a man appeared on the beach. He was partially drunk and, with his unkempt dress and unshaven face, appeared more like a beast than a man. He was small, dirty, uncouth. The frantic mother, as she could speak no Spanish, pointed to her daughter. He seemed at once to understand what had happened. Without waiting for a word he picked up the young woman and carried her into the house.

"If you wait for a doctor," the man said in Spanish, "he cannot reach you in time. Anyway, they do not know what to do. If you will let me help you, you will live. If you wait for a doctor, you will die."

Esther nodded assent. The rescuer rushed from the house. They discovered later that he was a pearl-diver living nearby, whose knowledge of the sea and sea animals had been learned from experience. In what seemed to the waiting women an endless time the man returned with a can of boiling tar and

121

a stick. It was heroic treatment. While the mother held the girl he poured liquid tar into the ragged wound and pressed it in with the stick. Esther screamed again and again, frenzied with the pain. The man took a bottle of cognac from his pocket and quickly forced some between her lips.

The day prior to the departure of mother and daughter to this beach cottage Miss Piper had sung for the group in the Institute living-room. As Dr. Montano meditated upon being separated from her for these vacation days he asked himself for the first time what it would mean, after these unbelievably happy hours, for them to drift apart at last, and life for him to drop back to the dull level of a Protestant monk's solitude. However, he now had an excuse to write to her. The sacred poetry of those first letters cannot be revealed. To his great joy she answered. Becoming bolder, he wrote of love. Her answer covered him with shame and confusion—but she *had* answered. Only one as ignorant of the things of the heart as Walter Manuel would have determined, as did he, never to mention that subject again.

Word of Miss Piper's accident came on Saturday. Dr. Montano's first impulse was to go to her side at once. But Mrs. Strachan refused to release him from his preaching engagement on the following Sunday. A few days later, however, he managed to meet mother and daughter at the halfway station upon their return trip. Now more than ever he felt that she must be, that she alone could be, his future companion. But also, more than ever, he felt that this could never be.

As it was vacation time at the Institute, Mrs. Piper and the daughter had the place very much to themselves. Their rooms opened out on to an upstairs porch overlooking a *patio* filled with tropical trees and shrubs which were covered with gaudily-coloured flowers. The mother extended a hearty invitation to Dr. Montano to visit them. Here on the veranda, seated in easy-chairs, they would watch the brilliant gold of the evening sky turn to fire against the green and blue of the distance, leaving the clouds with that mysterious colour sheen of early twilight which takes one's breath with the conviction of the presence of the divine Artist. Soon moon and stars would appear rising high above the far-away mountains where the Volcano Poas lifted his fronded heights to the soft embrace of the night.

Here it was that that question of all questions was asked. For him it was inevitable. For mother and daughter it became the main topic of conversation. Should Esther say the final "yes"? What might it mean for the future? What would friends in the homeland say? And yet, what could they say? Where among them would one find his culture, refinement, and evident devotion to Christ? Perhaps this mystic call of love was beckoning her to that career of service which the Master had planned. The essential problem after all was, is it God's will? The rest could be left to Him. Together they faced all possibilities—together they found the answer, God's answer.

Dr. Montano's father wrote when the news of the engagement was received, "Are you ashamed of your own people that you must marry a foreigner?" His uncle, mayor of Cochabamba, was very angry.

Now the really important part of this story is that on December 26th, 1928, Walter Manuel and Esther plighted their troth one to the other in the chapel of the Costa Rica Bible Institute. Rev. William L. Thompson, well-known missionary and author, acted as best man, and Dr. Strachan, according to Latin custom, after performing the ceremony preached a marriage sermon.

The next day they sailed for Peru.

CHAPTER EIGHTEEN

AT HOME IN INCA LAND

A FEW years before Dr. Montano's conversion the Catholic priests had made a determined fight to consecrate Peru to "the sacred heart of Jesus". Their success would mean that Roman Catholicism would become the State religion and all others forbidden. Haya de la Torre, one of the great youth leaders of the world, united the students and labourers of Peru in a protest against this action, which he considered a blow at the civil liberties of the people. Enraged at this opposition, Dr. Montano, then a Roman Catholic mouthpiece, from the seclusion of his monk's cell had written many articles against this political firebrand. Feeling ran so high between them that upon a chance meeting on the street they almost came to blows.

A little later Haya de la Torre disappeared and failed to return for many years. He had been taken prisoner and deported from the country. In preparation for further activities in Peru he had wandered from land to land, studying political philosophies, methods of labour and youth action, and the technique of organization on a large scale. During this period he went to Costa Rica, where, to his surprise, he met Dr. Montano, now an evangelical teacher and preacher, and the two became very warm friends.

One night these two young leaders of Latin America talked of spiritual things. The converted monk told of his experience in finding peace and salvation. Haya de la Torre also revealed his experiences when, as a boy, he was educated by the Jesuits, but found, as he grew older, that he was being spiritually and morally deceived. That night Dr. Montano gave his friend a Bible, which he was destined to carry with him until his return to Peru, where he was thrown into jail, while a number of his followers suffered martyrdom. During this imprisonment a letter, written on brown wrapping paper, was smuggled out to Dr. Montano, which later found a place in that splendid missionary book, *That Other America*, by Dr. John A. Mackay, which read in part:

"I should like to have a Bible. I have only with me a New Testament. I left my Bible among my books, and sometimes I miss it very much, for I am a regular Bible reader, and I like to see again many parts I am devoted to."

Thus, it was that during his stay in Costa Rica. Dr. Montano touched intimately, through its leader, Haya de la Torre, that great liberal movement in South America known as *Aprista*, which has been called "the highest point to which political thought, ethical idealism, and mystic fervour have ever attained in Latin American history".

But this contact with Haya de la Torre in Costa Rica resulted in Dr. Montano's writing an article for the Press severely criticizing President Augusto Leguia of Peru. The Peruvian missionaries felt considerable alarm at the possibility of Walter Manuel's returning to South America, and wrote warning him not to do so. The young man went to interview the Peruvian Consul in Costa Rica. "Is there any opposition on the part of the Government to my returning to Peru?" he asked. There was none. The missionaries went to the Peruvian Secretary of State and were informed that Dr. Montano was in no way *persona non grata*. Now that he was returning with a wife it seemed necessary to take every precaution; hence a letter was dispatched directly to President Leguia, giving a clear testimony of his deception in the Roman Catholic Church, his conversion to Jesus Christ, and his desire to preach the gospel in Peru.

Against every hope President Leguia responded most favourably and stated, "I congratulate you for the Christian sentiments of your letter. If you come to work here in Peru you and your wife will have the fullest protection of my Government." So the promise was fulfilled, "Behold, I set before you an open door."

The young couple arrived in Lima on January 15th, 1929, and Dr. Montano began his work as a representative of the American Bible Society in Peru. He was also called upon to hold evangelistic campaigns throughout the land and in neighbouring countries. Only once during this first year was he threatened with violent persecution. In Huancayo he was thrown into jail, accused of being a communist. When he produced the letter from President Leguia he was at once given his freedom.

At the close of 1929 Dr. Montano accepted an invitation to work with the Evangelical Union of South America. After a period spent in Tarma for the purpose of establishing the gospel in central Peru, he was called to Lima. Here at various times he helped to superintend one hundred and sixty self-supporting congregations in the surrounding territory; laboured among the Indians of the Andes; made extensive evangelistic tours, including a special ministry to the intellectual groups; carried on the Radio Church of the Air; was responsible for the evangelical periodical of the Evangelical Union, *Renacimiento*; assisted in establishing a Bible Institute, and acted as pastor of the First Peruvian Evangelical Church.

Then a much-needed furlough brought the family to the United States. Here, rest took the form of changed activities. There was a deputation work in English; evangelistic campaigns in Spanish-speaking Churches; a seven-months' pastorate in a large Mexican section of Los Angeles, California; two very strenuous evangelistic tours in Mexico; besides the preparation of articles for the religious Press and an extensive correspondence. It was here, too, that the great decision was made.

The lure of politics was one which no member of the Montano family could well resist. Very tempting offers reached him even while in North America. As a priest he could be a candidate for no public office. Papal excommunication had eliminated him from the priesthood, but he had not yet become an ordained minister. To do so would irrevocably shut him out from political life. One day while he was in the United States, after hours spent in prayer, he arose from his knees with that question for ever settled—God's way for him was not political activity, even though the presidency of his own country might be his. Shortly after this he took the vows of ordination in the First Presbyterian Church of Berkeley, California, while at the same time retaining his relationship as a missionary of the Evangelical Union of South America.

As we sit talking one afternoon with Dr. and Mrs. Montano in a Southern California bungalow, their daughter, Betty, six years of charm and mystery, suddenly bursts into the room, and spying the well-known visitor, calls out with true southern warmth, as she comes running, "Oh, Mr. Pearson, I love you! I love you!" "Junior", aged four, stands looking on rather tolerantly, a bit of a smile tucking in the corners of his mouth in a way which causes ladies who know him quite well to take him and shake him and hug him in unseemly fashion, all of which he endures with amazing composure and indifference. Edmund nestles in his mother's arms, than which no better place was ever found for a young missionary of nine months.

Dr. Montano is showing pictures and curios from Mexico, where programmes of round tables, addresses to literary and scientific societies, and constant evangelistic services have been declared by leaders to be the outstanding religious event of the year. Here there is a Presence as real as ever known by Galilee's shore. This is home—home like God meant it to be —the Christian home of the monk who lived again.

The hidden vista of the years ahead, how could he know it now? His was to be the joy of one day kneeling by his father's side to point him to the slain but living Lamb of God; of seeing brilliant men who once joined him to lead the "Students' Atheistic Association" publicly profess a saving faith in Christ; of churches, theatres, stadiums, and bull-fighting arenas crowded with men and women anxious to hear of a Saviour who could change despair to victory; of a brilliant platform ministry across North America which would deeply influence and mould the thought of the Church. All this and more, much more, was the "other story" yet to be told, that the best God does for a man is only a beginning, as has been proved in the life-story of "The Monk Who Lived Again".